CHIEF JOSEPH

Thunder-Traveling-over-the-Mountains
Courtesy of Azusa Publishing, LLC

Printed and Bound
in the United States
by Robert D. Bolen
Fort Boise Publishing
Nampa, Idaho

CHIEF JOSEPH & THE INDIAN WARS

ROBERT D. BOLEN

3

Palouse Indian Family
Courtesy of Wikipedia.org

ACKNOWLEDGEMENTS

First of all, I want to thank my wife, Dori for editing this book. She is excellent in English and grammar. Errors seem to vanish, when she looks them over!

I would like to express my deepest thanks to Teresa, owner of Azusa Publishing, LLC, in Denver, Colorado for all of the wonderful iconic Indian post cards that she has graciously allowed me to use in this text. The Curtis photos are superb. Pictures really make the book in my estimation. Her website ad containing gorgeous authentic Indian postcards is on page 180. I highly recommend her site.

I would also like to thank the Idaho State Historical Society for excellent pictures of Native Americans of long ago.

Thank you to Bonnie Fitzpatrick, my Graphic Designer for the wonderful job of creating the cover for this work. She does an excellent job. See her ad on page 181.

I have an additional source for photos and thank you so much, Wikipedia, who gave permission for the use of their photos and have allowed me the use of their gallery.

Last, but not least, my sincerest thanks to Ingram Publishing Company for their professional job of printing this fine publication.

the Author

CONTENTS

ILLUSTRATIONS

7

PREFACE

Wild aborigines migrated across the Bering Strait to the continent of North America thousands of years ago. They came following huge herds of bison-bison buffaloes across the plains. The aborigines hunted the large game that was top of the food-chain and used the skins to construct tents for dwellings. They dwelled in caves, overhangs, and pit-houses. The majority of peoples were hunters and gatherers. Men hunted and fished. The women dug roots and picked berries. The women crafted baskets and made pottery. They scraped hides and made the clothing.

American Indians did not own land per se, but dwelled in territories, which contained lands, creeks and rivers. They migrated seasonally in rounds to obtain food by fishing, hunting and gathering.

When enemy tribes attempted to move onto their lands there was conflict. Indians painted their bodies with war paint made from berries and minerals. They painted and adorned their horses with feathers and went to war. They wore war-bonnets of eagle or hawk feathers. When scalping was introduced by the French, the Indians adopted the practice in war. The tribe scalped their fallen enemies and then did a scalp dance or victory dance.

The Spanish Expedition landed early on American shores. Columbus landed in the Americas in 1492. War with the Indians actually began along the East Coast, when Columbus and other Spanish explorers arrived on their soil. Hernan Cortez came to shore bringing modern horses to America. Spaniards treated the Pueblo Indians of the Southwest cruelly. In 1539, Francis de Coronado encountered violent resistance from the New Mexico Pueblo Indians.

In 1607, the Pilgrims landed on Plymouth Rock. The Indian, Squanto and his Patuxet tribe celebrated with them that first Thanksgiving. Thirteen colonies were formed. Colonists began migrating into Indian Territory of Alabama, Kentucky, Mississippi and Tennessee. Native Americans living in those regions were considered baggage for settlers wanting to farm.

In 1680, Pueblo Indian captives of the Spanish, rebelled and ran the Spanish colonists out. They fled the country. At this time Indians gained the horse left over by the Spanish. Thousands of horses became available to the Indians. Comanche Indians and other tribes captured and amassed thousands

8

of horses and built large herds. They drove huge herds of horses north and supplied the Indians of the Pacific Northwest. The Plains Indians fought to protect their traditional lands. The fierce Blackfeet, Comanche and Sioux, for instance, drove other smaller tribes from their lands.

The Indian Removal Process had already begun after 1800. In 1800, the Choctaw Indians agreed to accept land in Oklahoma Territory. Many tribes had been forced to move westward by white settlement in the Indian territory across the Mississippi.

The Louisiana Purchase was negotiated in 1803 from France. President Thomas Jefferson dispatched the Lewis and Clark Expedition to explore the wilderness west of the Mississippi to the Pacific Ocean. The Lewis and Clark Expedition fought with the Blackfeet Indians in 1805.

By 1810, some of the Cherokee Indians had moved out and in 1817 larger migrations followed. In 1818, a treaty by the Osage Indian Tribe completely opened northeastern Oklahoma and added land to the public domain. Arkansas became a territory in 1819. The Cherokee accepted a land exchange in Oklahoma in 1820. Settlers also crossed the Mississippi. Mississippi became a state in 1821.

During 1820 dozens northeastern, Midwestern and southern tribes were forced to leave their homes under the Indian Removal Act. These tribes were forced to cede their lands and move west.

In 1825, another treaty adjusted the eastern boundary of the Choctaw. The Cherokee resented being surrounded by settlers. The same year, President John Quincy Adams and Secretary of War John C. Calhoun developed the idea of an Indian Territory in Kansas, Nebraska, parts of Iowa, and Oklahoma.

The Cherokee Indians wrote their own language and in 1827 they created their own constitution, modeled after that of the United States. During the time period from 1828-35, they published a newspaper, called the Phoenix, in the Cherokee Indian language and English.

In 1828, the federal government conducted another treaty with the Cherokee Indians to move west of the line. The settlers remained east of the line. The same year, the Cherokee and Choctaw Indian nations was resurveyed along the Arkansas-Oklahoma border.

The Indian Removal Act was signed into law May 28, 1830, by President Jackson. The act authorized him to grant unsettled lands west of the Mississippi River for Indian lands within eastern state borders. Some tribes went peaceably; others resisted.

George Catlin, famous artist who wrote about the Indians, estimated the Comanche's numbers to be 30-40,000 in 1830. They had endless resources from millions of buffalo and tens of thousands of antelope and wild horses.

Indian Nations were declared sovereign in order to be able to cede land, based on Georgia law of 1830, which prohibited white settlers from trespassing on Indian lands. The American Indians could occupy land, but not hold title to it.

The Georgia Supreme court, in 1831, declared that Cherokee Indians had the right to self govern, but Jackson refused to enforce it. He regarded the Indians as children, needing guidance and believed that the Indian Removal Act would protect the Indians and allow them to govern themselves in peace. Missionaries that aided in resisting removal were lawfully removed. Some of the citizenry protested against Indian removal and said that it was a brutal and inhumane treatment of the Indians.

Mexico banned trade with Comanche tribe in 1831. In 1832, the Comanche caught enemy Pawnee Indians stealing horses and killed all of the Pawnee. In 1834, Mexico renegotiated peace with the Texas Comanche Indians; then the same year dishonored the settlement and the Comanche warriors resumed their raids on the Mexicans.

In 1834, a region of Oklahoma was established as "Indian Territory." A former possession of the United States in eastern Oklahoma, Indian Territory covered 31,000 square miles.

In 1834, the U.S. government stepped in to stop the war and negotiated a peace between the Comanche Indians and the eastern tribes. The Comanche signed, but not willingly, because of others living on the outskirts of their territory; yet they respected the agreement.

Natives of that region were in disagreement about giving up land to the eastern intruders, the Comanche Indians, in particular. Eastern tribes settled on Comanche hunting grounds and they went to war.

Sonora, Chihuahua and Durango, Mexico established bounties for Comanche scalps. The Comanche Tribe signed a treaty with the American government in 1835, but still raided tribes for horses.

In the autumn of 1838-39, the U.S. government made the Cherokee Indians trek on a forced march cross country over The "Trail of Tears" to Indian Territory in Oklahoma; 4,000 Cherokees died on the long journey.

In 1840, a peace treaty was bartered between the Comanche, Kiowa and Kiowa-Apache Indians and with the Cheyenne and Arapaho tribes.

Trade with the Indians was government regulated and the white settler was excluded from negotiating. At that time, Kansas, Missouri, and southern Oklahoma to Arkansas made up Indian Territory.

The southern tribes of Chickasaw, Creek, and Seminole Indians were also forced to migrate to Indian Territory. The Delaware, Kickapoo, Miami, and Shawnee were removed into present day Kansas by 1840. The Indian Territory had been populated, but not as a confederation.

About 1842, the wagons rolled westward along the Oregon Trail. Euro-Americans, who ventured out West, were explorers, artists, gold miners, missionaries, ranchers, soldiers, and trappers. Pioneers started their westward expansion and began to travel on the Oregon Trail by the hundreds. Wagons left St. Louis for Oregon Territory along the Oregon Trail, in 1843. Settlers by the thousands moved in a mass departure to obtain farmland and a new life.

President Grant wanted to instate the Indian Commission under the U.S. Army. Comanche Indians were a proud race, bold and daring. The socio-political structure of the Comanche warriors was a military one. The horse-mounted Comanche army was nearly unbeatable.

Settlers moved into Comanche Territory (Comancheria) on their way west to Oregon and California; Comanche warriors did not welcome strangers. Thousands of miners moved onto Comanche territory during the California Gold Rush in 1848. In the Gold Rush of 1849, Asiatic cholera was introduced to the Southern Plains. The Comanche and Kiowa Indians lost over half of their populations to white man's diseases.

The Indians became riled at the sight of thousands of white men crossing their territory. Out West, the Indian Wars began around 1850. Word of one Indian tribe going to war quickly reached other tribes and caused them to rebel. It became a contagion. Allied tribes fought the U.S.

Army. During the Civil War 1861-1865, the Indian Wars were being fought west of the Mississippi, while the Army and top generals were committed to the battle with few soldiers to serve on the western front. It is a relatively unknown fact that over 28,000 American Indians fought on the sides of the Union and the Confederate Armies.

The Comanche Indians fought to regain territory for their tribe and were not about to let go of it. The Comanche warriors fought any intruders that encroached on Comancheria. The Spanish and Mexican governments, settlers, the Texas Rangers and the U.S. Army all fought the Comanche.

The U.S. Army retaliated with a raid on an encampment or larger village of Comanche Indians killing women and children. In turn, a Comanche war party would seek revenge by massacring a white settlement. Enmity grew between them in a vicious circle. The Army used every means of defeating the Indians: ambush, disease, massacre, killing off the buffalo, reduction of land, warfare et cetera.

Nebraska and Kansas had fertile lands desirable for farming and soon became organized into states. Kansas entered the Union in 1861 and Nebraska in 1867. After the Civil War ended in 1865, the Indians were pushed even farther south in Oklahoma Territory.

The Indians east of the Mississippi River were conquered by the U.S. Army and forced to relinquish millions of acres of land to the United States government and were pushed off their land. White settlers pressured the government to acquire Indian lands for their crops and homes. Indians were moved west of the Mississippi into Indian Territory.

As part as the Jefferson Plan, all Indian peoples were to be relocated from the eastern United States to Indian Territory. These Indians were told that region would be theirs. The government moved the eastern tribes into Comancheria in Indian Territory in Oklahoma and they were given better provisions than the Plains Indians, who resented the intrusion.

The Five Civilized Tribes were hesitant to take possession of assigned lands, due to Comanche raiding parties. The Creek, Cherokee, Chickasaw, Delaware, and Seminole Indian tribes were honored by being called, "the Five Civilized Tribes." Most of these had slaves and were forced to free them after the Civil War. These eastern tribes were given land west of the Mississippi River. As the foreign Indian tribes moved in from the east, settlers moved onto their lands. The government took Comanche lands in exchange for the reservation.

Their total population was 884,507 people and they were given 19,475,614 acres at the time, averaging 230 acres for every man, woman and child. They resisted by holding onto their land from sale to the government. They adopted large-scale farming, to comply with government demands.

There was much corruption in the government. Finally a new Indian Commission was formed. The Indian Commission had joint jurisdiction with the Department of the Interior over Indian affairs and appropriations.

First, the Spanish Explorers arrived and then French Trappers. The Comanche traded horses to them. Spanish and Mexican soldiers came from the South. Texas Rangers, vigilantes and the U.S. Army fought the Comanche.

Oklahoma Territory, including Comancheria was opened up as Indian Territory and the Eastern Tribes arrived. The Comanche had not formed one complete tribe until the reservation days, but they loosely formed separate autonomous nomadic bands.

In 1845, the Republic of Texas became a state and was backed by the federal government. The Comanche Indians became an even more powerful adversary; as over 70,000 Americans rushed into Texas. Much of Comancheria had been settled by Euro-Americans by 1855.

The Comanche Indians consented to a reservation, between the Red and Washita Rivers. The "Treaty of Medicine Bow Lodge," was signed in 1867 by the Apache, Arapaho, Cheyenne, Comanche, and Kiowa Indians. They were to be provided annuities, churches, and schools in return. The tribes were to allow the "Iron Horse," locomotives to cross their land, cease raiding and agree to live on the reservation. 60,000 square miles (38.5 million acres) were given up for the three million acre (4,800 square mile) reservation.

Nowadays, the Comanche Nation Headquarters is in Lawton, Oklahoma. Their annual Homecoming powwow is held in Walters, Oklahoma. The Comanche Nation Fair is held every September.

13

George Catlin Paintings of the Comanche
Photos Courtesy of Wikipedia.org

CHAPTER ONE
THE CAYUSE WAR

French Canadians that trapped for furs in their territory named the tribe "Cayuse," derived from a French word designating the tribe. Cayuse in French meant an American Indian pony. The Cayuse Indian name for themselves in their tongue was Liksiyn. The Cayuse nomads dwelled on their lands at the confluence of the Snake, Umatilla, and Walla-Walla rivers with the Columbia. The Cayuse occupied territory from the Blue Mountains to the Deschutes River in present day Oregon and Washington. The Cayuse was a small Great Basin tribe that lodged in teepees along the Walla-Walla River in what is now northeastern Oregon. They were fishers, hunters and gatherers and brave warriors, enemies of the Snake Indians.

The Cayuse Indians were skilled as horsemen and breeders of fine ponies; they developed the Cayuse pony. The Cayuse bred horses for hunting and war, especially for endurance and speed. A small Indian horse of a solid color in the North and Northwest was called a Cayuse pony. The Cayuse became horse brokers and had large horse herds.

The region included the Cayuse, Flathead, Nez Perce, Walla-Walla, and Yakima Indians. These tribes subsisted on fish, game and roots. The Cayuse Indians dwelled next to the Nez Perce and Walla-Walla Indians and had a close association with them. The Cayuse and Nez Perce intermarried and learned each others' language. The Cayuse language was an isolate.

Marcus and Narcissa Prentiss Whitman with Henry and Eliza Spalding traveled overland from New York, reaching Fort Boise Idaho in 1836. The Spalding and Whitman missionaries were Presbyterians. The Spalding and Whitman families came west with the idea of winning Indian souls for Jesus Christ. In 1836, they traveled along with the American Fur Company caravan down the Platte River, through the Rockies to South Pass, and continued down the Snake and Columbia rivers following nearly the exact path that would become the Oregon Trail. Whitman's was the first wagon to cross the plains; the broken down remnant was abandoned at old Fort Boise on the Snake River. The party was escorted to "Fort Vancouver" by Hudson's Bay Company employees. Narcissa and Eliza were the first white women to come to Oregon. Marcus Whitman had no idea what lay ahead.

15

The Whitman Spalding Oregon Trail Marker- These Missionaries came overland from New York to Fort Boise in 1836, the first wagon to cross the plains. The wagon broke down and was abandoned at the fort. Mrs. Spalding and Mrs. Whitman were the first white women to reach Oregon.

Photo Courtesy of Ned Eddins

Whitman also established another mission at Kamiah 50 miles northeast of Lapwai. Whitman and Spalding brought wagon loads of supplies to their missions from Green River, Wyoming, establishing a wagon route to Fort Walla-Walla. Dozens of wagon trains led by Marcus Whitman rolled west.

The Cayuse Indians initially accepted the Whitman's with open arms. Whitman chose Cayuse land to build on. The Cayuse and Nez Perce tribes were both friendly to the missionaries at first. Whitman was a handsome, dedicated, hard working medical doctor. He married Narcissa Prentiss, a bright pretty school teacher.

The site they chose was on fertile ground in a forested region on Cayuse Indian land. The Mission grew to include a large adobe house, several residences, a gristmill and a blacksmith shop. In 1836, Reverend Marcus Whitman and his wife, Narcissa founded the Whitman Mission (Waiilatpu), place of the Rye Grass, seven miles west of present day Walla-Walla, Washington. Marcus established the Whitman Presbyterian Mission for the Cayuse Indians, 25 miles east of Fort Walla-Walla.

In 1836, Henry Spalding established the Lapwai Mission at the mouth of the Clearwater River among the Nez Perce Indians in Oregon Territory to convert the Indian people to Christianity. Spalding was an embittered complaining sort; his wife was plain and austere. Spalding's mission was the first Nez Perce settlement. It was 12 miles north of Lewiston in Idaho Territory along the river. He imported a printing press in order to print the New Testament into the Nez Perce language.

Marcus Whitman and the Indians had their problems early. The wild Cayuse Indians clashed with Whitman usually over money or whiskey. Whitman wished that the Indians would plant crops and become like white people. The men helped plant the crops and build structures and fences around the fields. The missionaries were provided with horsemeat from the Indians until the crops were harvested.

Observing the Cayuse tradition that the women did all of the work, Narcissa Whitman attempted to change that custom. She lit into the tribal chief, embarrassing him. He demonstrated that he could do some of the work. Chief Tilaukait was reported to have been very impulsive and had a hot temper. He was chief of the very tribe that they were there to save.

In 1837, Whitmans only child was born, a baby girl they named Alice Clarissa. Since she was born on Cayuse land, the Indians called her Cayuse-te-mi (Cayuse girl). On one occasion, Narcissa refused a gift of a pair of coyote paws from Chief Tilaukait, which angered him. The tribe was delighted when the child was born until the two year old toddled into the Walla-Walla River behind the mission and drowned in 1839, upsetting the tribe.

In 1842, Agent White arrived with more emigrants without soldiers for protection, money or goods. Later that year the American Board of Commissioners for Foreign Missions decided to close the Oregon Missions. In October Whitman started back East to try and keep the missions open crossing the Blue Mountains reaching Fort Hall backtracking from Fort Benton and Santa Fe. In 1843, he joined a trading company, en route to St. Louis. He arrived to seek monies on which to build the mission, but was advised to abandon the idea. Whitman sold his New York home to raise money and left New York on horseback with pack animals.

Reaching the Platte River in Nebraska Territory, Whitman joined emigrants bound for Fort Walla-Walla and headed up a massive wagon-train opening the Oregon Trail, called "the Great Migration." He wrote to James Porter, Secretary of War, saying he had piloted one thousand settlers with 120 wagons, 700 oxen and 800 cattle to Oregon in 1843 and stopped at Fort Boise to purchase coffee and flour from the Hudson Bay's Company at 50 dollars per hundred weight spending $2,000.

Whitman had promised the Cayuse Indians monies for land in 1836 that was never paid and hostilities arose. In 1843, in his absence, when Doctor Whitman did not keep his promise to pay them, the Cayuse warriors vandalized the mission during his absence and burned down a grist mill and outbuildings.

The Nez Perce tribe demonstrated at Lapwai, but during the massacre, Nez Perce Indians had harbored Dr. and Mrs. Spalding, to save them. Mrs. Whitman fled to Fort Walla-Walla and was later escorted home by the Hudson's Bay Company employees after Rev Whitman arrived in the early autumn of 1843. When Whitman returned from back East, he still did not have the money owed them. Dr. Whitman was living dangerously.

Cayuse Warrior, 1910
Photo Courtesy of Legends of America

A peacemaker, Indian Agent White and Hudson's Bay Company employees spoke to the Cayuse and continued to Lapwai to parley with the Nez Perce chiefs. They smoked the peace-pipe, signing a peace treaty. Agent White gave the Indians garden tools to appease them. White went back to Fort Dalles and on to Astoria to make peace with the Indians.

James K. Polk became president in 1844 and advocated territorial expansion. He believed in the "manifest destiny" and expanding the West. In 1845, the United States annexed Texas, and Oregon. The Infantry was assigned to the Northwest.

Father De Smet was a famous missionary among the Indians. He made a vast impact on many Plains Indians preaching Catholicism. De Smet was famous traveling from village to village establishing missions among the Crows, Flatheads, Gros Ventres, Nez Perce, and Sioux to name a few.

Settlers in wagon trains continued to stop at the stage stop and way station alarming the Indians. Hundreds of pioneers came to the Mission a landmark and way station along the Oregon Trail. To make things worse, a new blight was upon them adding to their problems. Unfortunately, the wagons carried measles. People at the mission began to come down with the dreaded disease. Some people at the mission contracted the measles, but only a six year old died.

The Indians started dying one at a time from the measles. The Cayuse Indians were stricken by the epidemic. The Cayuse people lost half of their tribe to measles from contact with the Whitman mission. The Indians bathed in cold water to reduce the fever. Whitman had warned them against it, but the Indians bathed in cold water anyway to combat the high fever and died as a result.

The medicine man pointed the finger at Whitman, calling him evil and a devil. The Cayuse shaman blamed the deaths on Doctor Whitman and called for the death of the palefaces. The Cayuse Indians were sure that the doctor had cast some kind of spell on them.

Jim Bridger had sent his six year old daughter, Mary Ann (the grand-daughter of Chief Washakie and daughter of Jim Bridger and Mary Washakie) to school at the Whitman Mission in Washington. By the time she was eleven years of age she had grown into a beautiful young woman.

As the Whitmans attended the sick November 29, 1847, Mary Ann was in the kitchen setting the table, when the Cayuse Indians burst in. Chief

Tilaukait, who had been a friend, and Tomahas, another Cayuse, entered demanding medicine. Tilaukait accosted Marcus Whitman and cried out that his third son had died of measles. Tomahas pulled his tomahawk from under his blanket and bludgeoned the Doctor from behind with a blow to the skull, killing Whitman instantly. Mary Ann screamed and fell out of the kitchen window; she cried out and ran around the house to the other door. Mary Ann ran in and screamed, "They are killing father." The women and children ran upstairs, but the Cayuse ordered them to come back down.

A Cayuse war-party had ambushed the mission. Marcus and Narcissa Whitman and nine others were murdered that day and two lay dying. The frenzied Cayuse killed fourteen settlers in all and torched the buildings. The women and children were captured, yet thirteen of them escaped to Lapwai mission; others made it to Fort Vancouver. During the massacre the Spaldings were protected by the Nez Perce Indians. One man escaped, but drowned en route to Fort Walla-Walla.

Forty nine women and children were taken captive by the Indians, but were later released. Mary Ann Bridger was taken along with the other hostages to Willamette Valley, but she died a year later possibly of exposure. The Cayuse held the prisoners as slaves. Then, the Hudson's Bay Company traded goods to the Cayuse in exchange for the captives. Forty nine prisoners survived. The Hudson's Bay Company brokered 62 blankets, 63 cotton shirts, 12 Hudson Bay rifles, 600 loads of ammunition, 7 pounds of tobacco and 12 flints for the return of the captives.

The Whitman Massacre was the beginning of the Cayuse War. The Cayuse initiated the Indian Wars in the Pacific Northwest. During 1848-49 the Cayuse Indians hid in the Blue Mountains. A civilian, Cornelius Gilliam, led 500 white settlers to attack the Plateau Indians, in retaliation for the Whitman Massacre. The mission was closed down.

A story told about Jim Bridger: A small band of angry Blackfoot Indians who disliked him trapping animals on their lands was in hot pursuit of Bridger. His horse became lathered as he rode for his life in his retreat, his horse in a full gallop. Jim headed for his fort, kept his scalp and managed to stay alive, but caught an arrow in the back. He survived with the arrowhead in his backbone. Finally three years later, Marcus Whitman removed the arrowhead without using anesthetic.

Cayuse Chieftain Umapine 1909
Photo Courtesy of Wikipedia

In 1848 California, New Mexico, and Texas, were added to the American boundary increasing the size of the U.S. by 1,000,000 square miles. In 1849, a gold strike brought thousands of miners.

In the autumn of 1849, the Cayuse Indians handed over five Indian fugitives that had participated in the massacre. Arrested were Kimasumpkin, Klokamas, Isaiachalkis, Tilaukait, and Tomahas. All five were convicted and hanged in 1850 for the murder of the Whitmans.

Treaties were signed in 1854, west of the Cascades; the governor hoped to have had the Indians moved onto reserves by June 1855 and held the Walla-Walla Council. Three treaties were signed for the Northwestern Plateau. The Cayuse tribe ceded its traditional lands to the U.S. government in 1855 by treaty and transitioned onto the Umatilla Reservation; they formed a Confederated tribe. The Cayuse have resided there ever since. In 1855, the Cayuse joined the treaty with the Umatilla and Walla-Walla Indians when the Umatilla Reservation was established.

In the first treaty, Cayuse, Umatilla and Walla-Walla tribal lands were reduced from four million acres to 95,000 acres. In the second Treaty, fourteen tribal groups agreed to go to the Yakima Reservation. The third treaty confined the Nez Perce to their reservation in parts of Idaho, Oregon, and Washington Territories.

In July of 1855, the Flathead Council produced the Flathead Treaty and ceded Flathead, Kutenai and Upper Pend d'Oreille Idaho and Montana lands to the United States. Three tribes were to go the Montana reservation. Presently, the Cayuse Indians share a reservation with the Umatilla and the Walla-Walla tribes as part of the Confederated tribes of the Umatilla Indian Reservation. The reservation is located near Pendleton, Oregon.

The Cayuse elders spoke at the Cayuse Delegation Treaty of 1855. "We love our country. It is composed of the bones of our people and we will not part with it." The Federal Government forced the Cayuse onto the Umatilla Indian Reservation and ceded Indian territories were declared Public Domain causing conflict with the settlers, who had begun moving onto Cayuse land. G.H. Abbot was ordered by the Indian Department and forced by settlers under threat of hanging Indians to move the Cayuse, Umatilla, and Walla-Walla people to their reservation. Bootleg liquor, horse theft and other complications caused the Superintendent of the Umatilla Agency problems.

Yakima Warrior
Photo Courtesy of Wikipedia.org

CHAPTER TWO
THE COEUR D'ALENE, PALOUSE, SPOKANE & YAKIMA WAR

The Palouse (Palus) dwelt along the Columbia, Palouse, and Snake Rivers that include parts of northern Idaho, northeastern Oregon, and eastern Washington on the Columbia Plateau, where their traditional lands were. They depended mostly on fishing for their sustenance, although they relied partially on hunting and gathering.

The Palouse and Yakima were Sahaptian speakers in the same family as the Nez Perce. The Spokane and Coeur d'Alene spoke the Salish dialect. They were able to communicate by way of Indian sign language.

The Palouse Indians lived in three major villages: the Lower, Middle, and Upper Palouse bands. Palouse were breeders and raisers of the fine Appaloosa horses with the spotted hind quarters; the Appaloosa was named after the Palouse tribe. Palouse assisted the Lewis and Clark Expedition along the Snake River on their trek to the Pacific Ocean in 1805.

On May 17, 1858, the Coeur d'Alene, Spokane, and Yakima Indians attacked a column of U.S. Army regulars under Lieutenant Colonel Edward Steptoe from Fort Colville. Lieutenant Colonel Steptoe led 152 enlisted men, five company officers and two other officers, a total of 160 men with three Nez Perce Indian scouts. The attack came at a time that the Northwest Indians were besieged by farmers, fur traders, miners, and ranchers, who wanted their territory. Thirty civilians tended the pack train of cattle, horses and mules. Nez Perce Chief Timothy and his band assisted Steptoe's envoy crossing the Snake River. The Palouse Indians refused to be forced onto reservations, but did join other tribes on reserves later on.

The men were inadequately armed with older muzzle-loading rifles and approximately 40 rounds per man, nearly impossible to load on horseback. Company officers carried Colt Dragoon revolvers. They had two Mountain Howitzers that proved to be useless. Horse-mounted warriors could avoid their fire.

The Dragoons were ordered to leave their sabres behind, reducing the effectiveness of a charge. The Indians were alarmed because the U.S. Army column was so far east of the normal route northward to Fort Colville, where Steptoe was headed. Troop movement had frightened the Indians.

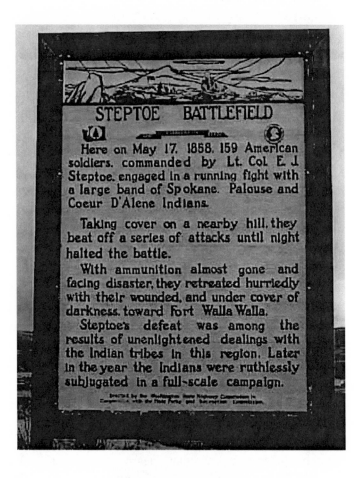

STEPTOE BATTLEFIELD

Here on May 17. 1858. 159 American soldiers. commanded by Lt. Col. E. J. Steptoe. engaged in a running fight with a large band of Spokane. Palouse and Coeur D'Alene Indians.

Taking cover on a nearby hill, they beat off a series of attacks until night halted the battle.

With ammunition almost gone and facing disaster, they retreated hurriedly with their wounded, and under cover of darkness. toward Fort Walla Walla.

Steptoe's defeat was among the results of unenlightened dealings with the Indian tribes in this region. Later in the year the Indians were ruthlessly subjugated in a full-scale campaign.

Steptoe Battle Monument
Monument to the Battle of Pine Creek in Rosalia, Washington
Photo Courtesy of Wikipedia.org

At the north end of Alpowa Creek, Lieutenant Colonel Steptoe was again aided crossing the Snake by Nez Perce Chief Timothy's band. It was normal for these Indians to become alarmed at this time. The Indians could defend their lands and were not afraid to fight any way that they could. The evening of May 15, 1858, Steptoe's unit camped alongside the west side of Pine Creek at a site called Tohotonnimme, beside the Nez Perce and Ingossomon beside the Palouse and Spokane Indians. It is just outside present day Rosaria.

The following day, a large number of painted Indians arrived to taunt the soldiers. War cries filled the air. Lt. Colonel Steptoe had made some very bad choices. The column moved past the creek tributary into a draw between two hills. The Indians demanded to know Steptoe's intentions not believing the military was peaceful. The Indians refused the Armies' use of canoes to cross the Spokane River and blocked their advance to Fort Colville. Steptoe retreated to Fort Colville the next day, May 17, 1858.

The command rose at dawn and rode back to Pine Creek. Jesuit missionary, Joseph Joset tried to intervene and defuse the situation, but to no avail. The fighting was sporadic, as the soldiers pressed ahead holding their fire. Bullets began striking the soldiers. The Indians cut them off, dividing the unit in two. Troops counter attacked to avoid being surrounded. Two officers were killed. During the fighting, the remaining troops formed a circle. The perimeter was guarded by staying low. A circle around the pack animals, dead and wounded saved them. The warriors charged several times, but were held back.

On September 1, 1858, Colonel George Wright returned for revenge. Wright headed a column of 190 Dragoons in reckless hot pursuit of the Indians through the Spokane Valley, burning their fields of food source of grain, dried fruit, and vegetables.

On September 9, 1858, Wright and his men found a huge herd of horses, numbering over 800 mustangs near Liberty Lake. They captured 100 ponies and slaughtered the rest. Bleached bones could be seen for decades along the river. Wright's column continued to the Cataldo Mission in northern Idaho, where they made a settlement treaty with the Coeur d'Alene. Wright sent word for the tribes to meet at Smyth's Ford on Latah Creek, September 24, 1858. One hundred seven chiefs from the Coleville, Palouse, Pend d'Orielle and Spokane tribes were present.

Coeur d'Alene Indian Chieftains
Courtesy of the Idaho State Historical Society

Cayuse and Sahaptian delegates meet with Commissioner of Indian Affairs, Washington D.C. Back row left to right: John McBain, Cayuse Chief Showaway, Palouse Chief Wolf Necklace, and Lee Moorhouse, Umatilla Indian Agent. In the front row sits Umatilla Chief Peo, Walla-Walla Chief Hamli, and Cayuse Chief Young Chief [Tauitau]. All the chiefs, but Showaway wear 1890s tribal garb.

Photo Courtesy Public Domain

General Canby
Photo Courtesy of Wikipedia.org

CHAPTER THREE
THE MODOC WAR

In 1852, Snake Indians had massacred a wagon train at Bloody Point murdering 65 immigrants and wounding many more. In retaliation, 41 Modoc Indians were massacred during peace talks.

Chief Howluck (pronounced Oualuck or Oulux) was a 6' 5" giant of a Paiute Indian. He was called "Bigfoot" because his moccasin print measured 14 ½ inches. Chief Howluck was blamed for a raid on Warm Springs Reserve in June of 1859, but Supt. Geary knew that he was innocent since Howluck had been seen camped on the Klamath Lake in 1859 at the time of the raid. Howluck led a band of Paiutes of about 100 warriors that ranged from Boise Valley to Klamath Lake to the Warm Springs vicinity.

General George R. Crook was ordered to assume command of the District of Boise in November of 1866 during the Snake War. It had been tough going for General Crook. He endured war in winter weather, rough terrain and opposition from his ranks. Crook had unreliable guides, also. General Crook discovered the Paiute Indian village of Chief Howluck (Bigfoot) on the Owyhee River in eastern Oregon.

His Scouts tracked the hostiles across eastern Oregon country to the east side of the Steens Mountains, where they located the camp of Chief Howluck. At first light, December 26, 1866 General Crook and his company of 1st U.S. Cavalry charged the sleeping village of Chief Howluck. As General Crook led the charge and shouted the command to advance, his horse spooked and bolted through the village putting him in danger. The Cavalry followed in pursuit of the general, directing accurate fire. Shots were fired; Howluck stood his ground. Paiutes taunted as soldiers directed fire at them. Braves fell to the ground; others hid behind rocks. Mid-day, the Indians fled.

Crook won the Battle of Owyhee River; one man was mortally wounded and one injured. Thirty warriors were killed and seven were captured. Soldiers captured horses and found a Wells Fargo mail bag in their possession.

The Paiutes suffered heavy losses. One month later, Crook fought one last engagement with the Indians. He ended the expedition due to harsh winter cold. Crook would defeat a mixed band of Pit River Snake and Modoc Indians in the Battle of Infernal Caverns in California.

Chief Howluck and 61 warriors were captured in eastern Oregon by miners in June of 1868. Bigfoot had been on the war trail four years and was tired of the fighting and ready to talk peace and transition onto the reservation.

Naturally, the Indian fought for his homeland, but lost the fight. Howluck was one of those warriors. One should not have expected him to have acted any differently. A military detachment from Fort Lyon wiped out a band of Paiute allies. Bigfoot and one hundred thirty Paiutes voluntarily entered the reserve. Chief s Howluck and Has-No-Horse became Reservation chiefs. Adaptation to the coming of the white man was hard for the American Indian to endure.

In 1864, the Modoc tribe signed a treaty and agreed to live on the Klamath Indian Reservation in Oregon. They dwelled there intermittently until April of 1870, but were unable to coexist peacefully with the Klamath Indians. The Modoc Indians left the reservation. The U.S. Army attempted to force Captain Jack Kientopoos and his band of 52 braves back to the Klamath Reservation. It was then that the Modoc War erupted on November 29, 1872. One hundred fifty Modoc Indians had been camped on the Lost River.

The Modoc Indians retreated to their stronghold, the lava bed outcroppings south of Tule Lake with its caverns and caves-an impregnable fortress, and assumed the defensive. The Army arrived with a complement of soldiers and artillery for battle.

The war lasted from 1872-1873. The Modoc War also called the Modoc Campaign or the Lava Beds War because the battle was waged in the lava fields. The Indians held out for months having the advantage by using the difficult terrain for cover.

The Modoc hostiles fought an ongoing battle against General Edward Sprigg. On January 17, 1873, in heavy fog, General Canby failed to dislodge the entrenched Modoc warriors and sustained heavy losses. The U.S. Army counted 35 dead and many wounded.

April 11, 1873, on Good Friday unarmed, Canby and another man were conducting peace negotiations, when they were murdered by Captain Jack and other Modoc warriors. Canby was the one general to die in the Indian Wars. Captain Jack thought the Army would retreat without their fallen leader, but he was wrong.

Modoc Chieftain, Captain Jack of the Modoc War
Photo Courtesy of Wikipedia.org

April 14, 1873, the U.S. Army under Jefferson C. Davis returned and attacked the Indian stronghold. Under siege, Captain Jack retreated for lack of water and fled to the south. On April 26, the Army unit under Davis pursued the Indians and rode into a Modoc ambush. Davis lost two thirds of his squad of 85 men. The Modoc Indians lost between 50 and 100 warriors.

Their days numbered, the Modoc Indians faced 1,000 army regulars plus volunteers. Short of guns, supplies, and badly outnumbered, Captain Jack's Modoc band began to desert. Warrior Hooker Jim split from Captain Jack's band and led several other warriors to the Fairfield Ranch, where he knew the rancher. Hooker Jim and his band then surrendered.

A Modoc war party under Captain Jack desperate for supplies and horses, attacked an Army unit at Sorass Lake on May 10, 1873. The Army suffered heavy losses and lost 24 pack mules and ammunition. Captain Jack retreated and escaped with only 33 remaining warriors from an Army trap of 300 soldiers at Sand Butte. His warriors began to surrender one by one. Reinforcements captured Capt. Jack and the last of his band.

On June 1, 1873, Captain Jack laid down his rifle, at last. Captain Jack and three Modoc braves were executed. Two were sentenced to life in prison. The remaining 53 Modoc warriors were sent to Indian Territory in Oklahoma and held there as prisoners of war until 1909. Some returned to the reservation in Oregon. The Modoc War cost half a million dollars and many lives; It was the last Indian War fought in California or Oregon.

Modoc Battleground Drawing
Photo Courtesy of Wikipedia.org

CHAPTER FOUR
THE RED RIVER WAR

In 1778, a Comanche war party attacked the village of Pueblo de Bucareli in Comanche territory and drove off 200 horses and destroyed the village. Spanish colonists killed three of the Comanche warriors.

Ten Bears, a Comanche chief also known as Ten Elks, born in 1792, was a leader of his people, an eloquent speaker and a peacemaker. He did not raid as a warrior. He was more a "peace chief" an elder in the tribe, held in high esteem. Ten Bears was voted as a delegate to represent the Comanche tribe, but gained no concessions from the government. He later visited the peace conferences in Washington D.C.

Chief Iron Jacket *(Pobishe Guasho)* was also a great chief of the Comanche Nation. He took the name Iron Jacket because he possessed a Spanish coat of mail. He claimed great powers to deflect the white man's bullets with his breath. Iron Jacket fathered a son, named *Pe-ta'-no-ko'-na.* Iron Jacket was the grandfather of a great chief, Quanah Parker.

Peta Nocona *(Petanokona) or* Nocona, was born in 1825. He became a Comanche chief on the Southern Plains greatly feared by the frontier settlers in Texas. Little is known of his upbringing, but he was chief over the fierce *Noconi* band of Comanche Indians.

Christopher Houston Carson was a famous mountain man and Indian fighter. He was born a tiny baby on December 24, 1809 and nicknamed Kit. Kit worked as an apprentice and a herder, which led him to Santa Fe and Taos, New Mexico, a town that became his home.

At the "1835 Rendezvous," Carson was challenged to a horse-mounted duel by a French fur trapper bully, named Shunar, over an Arapaho Indian maiden named, *Waanike.* He shot Shunar and won Waanike for his wife; she bore him two children, but died very young. Kit learned Indian customs, languages and to sign, trapping for furs in the Rockies. He became a revered Indian fighter. Carson hired on as a hunter for Fort Bent.

William Bent married a Cheyenne Indian named, Owl Woman. In 1828, Bent, his brothers and partner, Ceran St. Vrain, built an adobe trading post, known as Bent's Fort, on the north bank of the Arkansas River, in what is now La Junta, Colorado. The walls were four feet thick and 15 feet high with round bastions at two corners. Bastions had

Chief Quanah Parker
"The Greatest Chief of the Comanche Indians"
Photo courtesy of Azusa Publishing, LLC

cannons and cactus on the walls deterred scaling; dimensions were 135 wide x 180 feet long, providing defense from Indians and a supply base.

Bent's Fort was a stopover on the Santa Fe Trail, a trade route between Independence, Missouri and Santa Fe, New Mexico. Furs were traded by Arapaho, Cheyenne, Comanche, and Kiowa Indians. It was frequented by John C. Freemont and the U.S. Army soldiers stationed there.

Army Colonel Henry Dodge and an expedition of dragoons were accompanied by the early artist, George Catlin, in July of 1834 and rode along medicine Creek. They were greeted by the Wichita Indians. Sam Houston sent Joseph C. Eldridge into the same region to barter peace with the warring Comanche. Randolph Marcy recommended that the mountain be named Mount Scott for General Winfield Scott. Leading a company of soldiers, he also recommended a post be established there.

Then, in 1834, 60 years after the attack on the Spanish village of Pueblo de Bucareli, the John Parker family built their fort very close to that same location. The Parkers, a prominent Virginia family, settled along the Navasota River, 40 miles east of Waco. It was built as a stockade fort, around a cluster of homesteads by the Parker family and their neighbors, an outpost on the frontier, near present day Limestone County in eastern Texas. The Parker family made a big mistake settling in Comanche territory.

Arriving in Texas, Silas Parker joined the Texas Rangers and became an officer in 1835. Texas rangers were horse-mounted law officers that ranged the Texas frontier to protect the local citizenry between the Brazos and Trinity Rivers. Elder John Parker was a veteran of the Revolutionary War. Others fought beside Andrew Jackson in the Battle of New Orleans.

The Parkers were very religious people of the Baptist faith and planned to Christianize the pagan Indians. The Parkers believed that they were the elect and that it was God's will they possess the land. On the contrary, Chief Peta Nocona and the Comanche tribe believed that the "Great Spirit" created the land for them. The white eyes were encroaching on their land and that meant war. Elder John Parker, his wife, sons and their wives and children and neighbors established Parker's Fort as a defense against attack.

The Buffalo Wallow Fight of 1874
Between the Kiowa and the Army
Photo Courtesy of Wikipedia.org

Preparing for war, Comanche warriors prayed to their "Grandfather" (their god) for a successful raid. The Indians painted their faces, bodies, and their horses with war paint. They did the war dance for victory and armed themselves with bow and arrows, and rifles.

Late in May 1836, farmers L.D. Nixon, L.M.T. Plummer and James W. Parker left the fort to work in the fields, near the river, about a mile distant. Ben Parker was standing guard in a field, when he saw the Comanche war party of over 200 warriors. The surprise attack was subtle as the Indians displayed a white flag of peace while they slowly rode in, a ruse to throw the Parkers off guard. Lucy Parker, Mrs. Nixon (Sila's niece), most of the women, and children ran for the neighbor's farm when they saw the Comanche war party. The warriors confronted and surrounded Benjamin Parker. His body was riddled with Comanche arrows.

Although the fortress was built to ward off wild Indians, the Comanche war party, led by Chief Nocona broke down its defenses and ambushed the immigrants inside Fort Parker. Silas Parker ran to get his shot pouch. Warriors shot Robert and Samuel Frost as they tried to defend the women and children. Elder John Parker and Mrs. Kellogg attempted to escape, but were cut off. Cynthia's grandfather was scalped alive and dismembered. Before he died her grandmother was molested, then stabbed with a knife and left to die. The Indians killed Elder John and Grandma, Benjamin and Silas Parker, G.E., Dwight, Robert, and Samuel Frost that morning in the Fort Parker massacre. The frenzied warriors tore the place apart pillaging the fort. As they rode out, the Comanche shot a number of cattle. The attack was fast and furious. The raider's message to others was to stay out of their territory.

The custom was to acquire slaves on a raid. The Comanche captured two women and three children in the massacre: Rachael Plummer, who was pregnant, and her young son, James, Elizabeth Kellogg, Silas Parker's six year old son John, and his nine year old daughter, Cynthia Ann. Ranger Silas shot four Indians, but died trying to defend the women and children.

The Comanche warriors rode along the streams in their territory in order to hide their tracks to their village. The captives were divided among three bands. One band stole Rachael

Plummer and James Pratt. Another band captured Elizabeth Kellogg and the third band took captives Cynthia and John Parker. Rachael Plummer was beaten often by her mistress. When she reached her breaking point, she grabbed the femur bone of a buffalo and beat her tormentor senseless. She became well known to the Comanche as the woman who dared to fight back.

Comanche war parties attacked unprotected ranches on the frontier. The Indian braves burned houses and captured their women and children and sold them into slavery as small towns were raided. The Comanche Indians had become slave traders for profit. They rode across the border into Mexican settlements and took slaves of women and children there. Females were usually raped. Being accustomed to capturing females in raids for wives and slaves, Comanche braves captured Indian, Mexican, Spanish, and Texan women and children. Women captives, who were ransomed and returned to society, had blank looks on their faces with empty stares, resembling brain wash. Women captives were always raped, as per Comanche custom and became the property of the warrior abductor. If there was a question of ownership, she became property of the whole Indian band.

Occasionally, children were adopted. Slaves were treated either humanely or sometimes cruelly. Young women were taught to carry water and gather wood to be hauled to the camp lodges, like regular Indian girls. In over a 150-year period it has been estimated that more than twenty thousand slaves were captured by the Comanche. They killed more white men and took more slaves of them than any other American Indian tribe.

Mrs. Plummer was ransomed after twenty one months and rescued from the Indians, as her will was broken. In August of 1837, Rachael Parker Plummer was purchased from the Comanche by Mexican traders, who paid her ransom and saved her life. She had a long, grueling journey along the Santa Fe Trail to Santa Fe, a province of Mexico. Rachael was considered to be the first woman to travel the Santa Fe Trail and the first U.S. citizen to reside in Santa Fe. She was the only survivor of the massacre that lived to tell the story. In Santa Fe Rachael was sold as a slave to William and Mary Donoho, who were kind to her and took her in. She slept in a bed for the first time in nearly two years. She bore two children there. They raised $150, promised to send her home to her father, but it was the wrong time. On February 19, 1838, after a hard 19 month passage, Rachael Parker Plummer arrived at her father's home in Huntsville. She was gaunt and scarred by the Comanche. Sadly, Rachael died a year later.

Revolt broke out in Santa Fe and 2,000 Indians massacred a compliment of two hundred militiamen. The insurgents went on to behead the governor and parade his head through the streets on a pole. A district judge was put in stocks by the rebels and his body mutilated.

In 1840, Colonel Len Williams and a Delaware Indian guide visited the Comanche four years after Cynthia had been captured and had heard stories of a blue-eyed blonde female held captive in this village. Chief Pahauka let the Colonel see Cynthia. He tried to speak with her; she just stared at the ground, did not talk and ran and hid. Cynthia had made a decision to live, so she turned Comanche. Williams offered a ransom for the girl, but Pahauka, her Indian father, refused the trade saying it was not enough. Having grown fond of Cynthia, the Comanche adopted her into the tribe. She would have been around 13.

Chief Pete Nocona took Cynthia for his bride when she became eighteen years of age and gave her the name, Nadua (Someone Found). She was one of many wives, being that they practiced polygamy. It seems ironic that Cynthia Anne became the bride of the one whose war party killed her family. She must have blanked everything out.

In the Battle of Banderas Pass in Texas, Captain Jack Hayes and 40 Texas Rangers fought hundreds of wild Comanche Indians on the Banderas Road 15 miles south of Kerrville, in 1842. The Rangers headed up the Guadalupe River Valley. The Indians had reached the pass ahead of them. The Comanche lay in ambush for the Rangers, who rode into the ambush one-third of the way through the pass.

Suddenly, the warriors attacked, firing arrows and musket balls at the unsuspecting men. Confusion broke out. Some were shot from their saddles; horses reared and spooked, but Hays did not lose his cool. Trained in Indian fighting he told them, "Steady there boys; we can whip them, no doubt about that. Dismount, tie your horses, fight them afoot." The Tennessean was a seasoned Indian fighter.

Horse-mounted Comanche Warriors
Photo Courtesy of Wikipedia.org

The Rangers answered with their repeating rifles and new Colt pistols they could reload quickly. The fight changed to hand-to-hand combat. A Comanche Chief and one of the Texas Rangers circled each other in a deadly knife fight; they fought for a time lunging at each other. The Chief thrust his knife to stab the Ranger, but he stabbed the Comanche in the heart, killing him. The Indians withdrew to the north end of the pass and wailed all night for the dead, but disappeared by daybreak. Hays and the Texas Rangers returned to San Antonio.

Kit Carson signed up as guide for John C. Freemont and married Josepha Jaramillo, his true love, in 1843. For four years Carson and Freemont blazed the Oregon Trail.

Around 1845, Quanah Parker was born to Cynthia and Chief Nocona in a tipi in the Wichita Mountains. He was destined to become Chief of the Comanche Nation, firstborn of three children. His younger brother was named Pena, (sweet as honey), or Pecos, and a little sister, Topsana or Prairie Flower. Nocona was pleased with Cynthia for bearing him three offspring The Comanche suffered from a low birthrate; women were always in the saddle causing miscarriages and limiting childbirths.

Quanah rode on horseback with his mother, as a baby and was in the saddle, as soon as he learned to walk. He had a pony of his own and as a teenager, was an expert horseman and skilled archer in the use of the bow and arrow. He could wield a knife, spear and tomahawk. Young Quanah grew into a muscular six foot warrior with steel grey eyes. By the time that he was 15 years old, Quanah had counted coup by taking an enemy's life.

Government officials, P.M. Butler and M.G. Lewis located Cynthia Parker and her brother John in a Comanche village at the head of the Wichita River. They offered a king's ransom for her, goods plus $400-500.00 cash, but Cynthia only ran and hid from them in fear. By then, she was already married to Chief Nocona. August 8, 1846, they wrote to the Bureau of Indian Affairs, who had rescued one white and three Mexican youth, but couldn't save the Parker children.

Around 1850, De Shields and a party of white hunters met Cynthia Parker on the prairie along the Upper Canadian River and offered to pay her ransom; friends of the Parkers, they asked her if she wanted to return to her family. Cynthia pointed to her children and shook her head, no.

Although she could not speak English, Cynthia signed that she had children and a husband she loved very much.

In 1850, Chief Peta Nocona, Quanah and the *Noconi* (wanderers) band were hunting buffalo, making jerky and tanning hides, when 40 Texas Rangers and 21 U.S. Cavalry, under Captain Lawrence Sullivan Ross attacked. They took the Comanche village at Pease River by surprise. Ross was on the trail of Peta Nocona since the Parker massacre. They took captive a blue-eyed Caucasian girl, who spoke no English. She was Cynthia Parker, prisoner of the Comanche. Her Uncle Isaac was summoned to identify her as his niece. Isaac took her back to eastern Texas to live with the Parkers. She attempted to escape and return to the Comanche world, but was caught.

Quanah took Weakeah, daughter of Comanche Chief Yellow Bear and four more wives. He fathered 25 children all together. Quanah was just 25 when he led his first war party. He learned that he was a half-breed and came under scrutiny for it.

When his father, Peta Nocona died of an old injury, Young Quanah Parker initiated and organized a composite band of Comanche and became their head chief of the Quahadi (Antelope) band of the Comanche Indians. A band is a group within the tribe sometimes having a chief. The Quahadi were the fiercest Indian warriors on the Southern Plains.

Quanah had to be a good hunter and mighty warrior, and favorite of the people to become chief. It helped that he was a good speaker. Quanah led his own war party and managed to be able to execute raids and disappear to elude the Army.

Chief Quanah told the story passed down from legend of how his Shoshoni Tribe came to be called the Snake Indians. The neighboring tribes referred to the Shoshoni by using the universal sign language of a slithering hand motion. This described how the Snake Indians would vanish behind rocks like "Snakes going backwards" and reappear to fight again.

By 1850, the Comanche had amassed such large herd of horses, that they had a surplus. Estimates have been made of the Comanche Indians owning as many as 50,000 horses at that time. Commerce was lucrative among the Indian natives. They rode hundreds of miles to raid for horses. Comanche Indians built massive herds of horses, as tribal wealth. One warrior could own 250 horses. Quanah owned over 1,000 head of horses.

The Cheyenne Indians possessed beads, blankets, brass kettles, calico, guns, ammunition and horses garnered from bartering with the forts to trade. The Apache, Comanche and Kiowa Indians brought horses for trade with the southern Cheyenne Indians.

At the time of the Comanche massacre on Fort Parker, Kit Carson and Will Drannan were trading furs they had trapped in Comanche territory, in a village on the Arkansas River. They were experienced in fighting the Ute Indians.

In 1852, Chief Kiwatchee asked Carson and Drannan to join them in war against the Utes. Kit declined and said that he would rather observe the fight. The two tribes faced each other, while Comanche drum warriors beat tom-toms; the Comanche braves charged and fought in mortal combat. As the battle ended, the Comanche warriors had won. Comanche counted wounds as signs of valor.

In 1853, a number of Comanche warriors returned to their old haunts. The status of Comanche women had deteriorated, as agriculture was abandoned and warfare took its place as the norm. Gold miners in Colorado, 1850-60's clamored over Indian land, by the thousands. By 1858, tension ran high among the Indians.

Four South western Indian tribes banned together in a peaceful socio-political alliance against the white man. The allied tribes voted Quanah Parker, son of a Comanche chief, as their leader and war chief.

In 1860, Chief Quanah led the Comanche, Kiowa, Kiowa-Apache and Southern Plains Arapaho against the white-eyes. Chief Quanah, mounted on his black stallion, at the head of a band of several hundred whooping Indian warriors, struck fear in the eyes of the enemy.

In 1860, the U.S. Army sent three columns of troops to fight the Arapaho, Cheyenne, Comanche and Kiowa Indians, who had closed the Santa Fe Trail.

Cynthia Parker never adjusted to the way of life of the white man; heart-broken, she died in 1861. Her husband, Peta Nocona also died the same year, of an old wound. Their love evolved under very strange circumstances, but apparently was true love. Their deaths troubled Quanah and his brother, Pecos, also died of disease.

Chief Quanah's daughter, Wanada
Courtesy Western History Collections
University of Oklahoma Libraries

In 1861, Civil War began in America during Abraham Lincoln's presidency. Tragically, the south waged war against the north and brother fought brother. The war was fought mainly over slavery, which was favored in the south. Eleven slave states in the south had seceded from the Union; they formed the Confederate States of America or the Confederacy, led by General Jefferson Davis.

The Union, in the north was comprised of 23 Free States that had abolished slavery and 5 border-states. 700,000 soldiers died during the War Between the States. As the Civil War raged, the Indian Wars were fought in the southwest, while the Army and top generals were committed, with few soldiers on the western front.

With the Civil War over, the Army roles were greatly reduced down to 25,000 officers and enlisted men in 1869 left to fight the Indian Wars. The rag-tag U.S. Army was undisciplined. Half of the recruits deserted, rather than report to fight Indians.

The Comanche Indians were forced to sign away their lands and accept reservation life, but they preferred their old days and ways.

In 1863, there was a full-scale war on the Great Plains, with the fore-mentioned tribes plus the Kiowa-Apache. During the war on the Southern Plains, marauding Comanche and Kiowa war parties continued making vicious raids on white settlements. Quanah and his Quahadi band were relentless in their attacks.

Settlers were murdered, their women and children were captured for slaves and wives and their horses and livestock were stolen. Chief Quanah Parker led war parties into Mexico and raided there, taking captives. The Kiowa Indian war parties raided into Mexico also, under Chief Lone Wolf.

Aided by the horse, the Comanche army was nearly unbeatable as the "Lords of the Southern Plains." War leader of the combined tribes, Quanah and his braves entered into combat with the 4th Cavalry, the Spanish Army, Mexican Army and Texas Rangers in the Comanche Wars. At the same time they warred with other Indian tribes.

The U.S. Army appointed Colonel Carson to assemble the Navajo nation onto the Basque Redondo Reservation and by November of 1863, he only had recruited 200 Navajos.

The Navajo Indians in Canyon de Chelly were members of bands led by three chiefs, Manuelito, Barboncito and his brother, Delgado. Barboncito and Manuelito had vowed to never surrender. The two leaders led their bands to a rock formation, known as the Navajo fortress at the confluence of the Black Rock Canyon and Canyon del Muerto. The Navaho had stockpiled provisions enough to hold off an army. Colonel "Kit" Carson sent his troops in to both ends of the canyon to seal it off and defeat the Navajo nation. The destruction of the Navajo camps, crops, and supplies added to their demise. Cold, hungry, and tired, the Navajos made the long, tedious walk to Basque Redondo, known as the "Long Walk of the Navajos." By the summer of 1864, 8000 Navajos had transitioned onto the Basque Redondo reservation.

Carson rode dispatch to Washington D.C. Kit was appointed Indian Agent for the Ute Indians in New Mexico and served 10 years; they loved "Father Kit." During the Civil War, he had made Brigadier General. In 1864, Comanche and Kiowa Indians were attacking stage coaches, and wagon trains bound for Santa Fe. General James H. Carleton ordered Colonel Christopher Carson, in command of the 1st Cavalry of New Mexico Volunteers, into the interior to engage the warring Indians south of the Canadian River.

The first Battle of Adobe Walls occurred November 25, 1864, when Colonel Christopher "Kit" Carson engaged the Comanche, Kiowa and Kiowa-Apache in war. Kit built an army of 14 officers, 321 enlisted men, 75 Ute and Jicarilla Apache scouts and soldiers from Lucien Maxwell's ranch, at Cimarron, New Mexico. Lt. George Pettis was in command over 27 wagons, two howitzers, an ambulance and 45 days rations. Due to heavy snowfall, Carson left Lt. Col. Abreau over the Infantry and a supply train as back up.

Colonel Carson headed the march toward Adobe Walls, where there was a winter camp of Comanche and Kiowa Indians on the Texas panhandle, in the area Kit had worked at Bent's Fort 20 years earlier. His scouts reported a large body of Indians, horses and cattle mingling around Adobe Walls. No talking or warming cooking fires were allowed. On November 25, 1864 about 8:30 a.m., Carson's command attacked the Kiowa village of Chief Dohasan of about 150 lodges and routed them from their settlement. Word of the attack spread, as Carson moved his Army toward Adobe Walls. An encampment of 500 Comanche lodges and thousands of warriors was more than Col. Carson had imagined. Comanche warriors attacked, but Pettis' howitzers held them back. Chief Dohasan led many attacks, as did Chief Satanta and Chief Stumbling Bear. It must have been a comical sight to see Satanta in the army uniform General Custer gave him, answering Carson's bugler's call with a trumpet he stole from a fallen soldier.

Rations were running low and Colonel Carson called a retreat, knowing that they were outnumbered by several thousand Indians. The Comanche braves realized this and started brush fires, burning toward them to block their retreat. Carson countered by moving to higher ground, by lighting fires also and continued rifle fire.

Carson gave the order to burn the Kiowa and Kiowa-Apache lodges, as it turned twilight. Kiowa Chief Iron Shirt refused to leave his teepee and died in the fire. Robes, weapons and rations were destroyed in the fire. Colonel Carson continued his retreat. Low on supplies, he reconnoitered with Lt. Colonel Abreau's column from Mule Springs. The two forces united and camped for the night. The next day they rode to Fort Bascom and disbanded.

In four days Colonel Carson had won a great victory. The Indians lost around 150 warriors and 175 lodges. Carson's losses were three dead and 25 wounded; three died later. A young Mexican volunteer took an Indian's scalp. Carson fought 2,000 Comanche and Kiowa in the Texas panhandle area, second only in volume to George Armstrong Custer in 1876 at Custer's Last Stand. Carson's wife, Josepha, died and Kit followed one month later, in 1868. The Second Battle of Adobe Walls would occur in ten years.

Black Kettle had informed Fort Lyons of the area where his tribe's village was located, 40 miles north of Fort Lyons; he was a peace chief and had spoken to the Army of peace. He flew an American Flag and a white flag over his lodge. Black Kettle and his warriors were on a buffalo hunt. Five days after the Battle of Adobe Walls, on November 29, 1864, Colonel Chivington and 700 Colorado volunteers attacked and massacred the sleeping village of Cheyenne women and children. Chivington reported to Fort Lyons and was informed Black Kettle had already surrendered, but Chivington disregarded the news and rode ahead of his column toward Black Kettle's village. Black Kettle was chief of a band of 600 Southern Cheyenne and Plains Arapaho Indians. He thought they were at peace, but the Cavalry came. It was a cowardly act. Chivington knew this but massacred the village.

Angry war parties of Plains Arapahos and Southern Cheyenne Indian warriors killed a pioneer family outside of Denver during the Indian War called the Cheyenne–Arapaho War or the Colorado War of 1864-65. War parties attacked mining camps, stage-lines and wagon trains.

Colorado Territory Governor John Evans wanted the Indians' hunting ground for white settlement. The Indians refused to sell. Governor Evans asked Lieutenant Colonel John Covington to stop the Indian violence. Covington was known to hate the Indians, who wanted to see them eradicated. He enjoyed attacking Arapaho, Comanche, Kiowa and Sioux villages, razing them to the ground, in early Colorado and Kansas. The Treaty of Medicine Lodge was signed between the U.S. Army and the Comanche, Cheyenne and Plains Apache Indians, October of 1867.

Comanche warriors hunted and went on the war trail across the Texas frontier, religiously. Their hunting and going on raids clouded the perception of Indians living on the reservation. The idea of staying on the reservation and drawing winter rations from the agency, before going out during the summer to raid and hunt buffalo was not working. There was peace in winter and bloodshed in the summer. Comanche attacks in 1868 wiped out many American outposts. The U.S. Army answered by removing Indians from the plains.

The Indians complained of the lack of firearms to hunt to provide ample food, so the Department of the Interior delivered several tons of guns and ammunition to the Plains Indians, although it

The Great Comanche War Chief Quanah
Photo Public Domain

was illegal under federal law to sell guns to them. Many of the guns delivered were new-model repeating Spencer and Henry rifles, while the U.S. Army carried older single- shot models. The Plains Indians became better equipped than the Army, courtesy of the American government. Now they could hunt and raid to their heart's content.

Quanah led his Quahadi band and traveled far out on the Southern Plains to hunt the buffalo and avoided the white man, his culture, soldiers, settlements and disease. They made the exception and raided the settlements and stayed isolated, the best they could.

While some tribes raided from Texas into Kansas, Chief Quanah led war parties south into Mexico. Other Comanche bands waged war into Kansas and Texas. Federal law prevented the number of Indians arrests unless they were on reservations with the agent's permission.

They continued to fight the Ute Indians. They hunted the buffalo and traded the hides for guns and ammunition to the Mexican traders, who also provided the Comanche with a new ten-shot lever action repeating rifles. The Comanche Indians had progressed from the primitive bow and arrow to modern weaponry in a few short years. The repeating rifles were an advantage to the Comanche in war.

In 1874, a Comanche prophet named *Ishatai* (White Eagle), a Quahadi medicine man, had a vision of the white man being driven from the Southern Plains forever by Comanche warriors and the buffalo returning if they did the Sun Dance, which they had not done before. Warriors who danced the Sun Dance were supposedly given powers of resistance by the gods for protection from white man's bullets. White Eagle directed the Sun Dance. Several bands participated in the first and last Sun Dance in 1874. The ordeal was common among the Plains Indians. Comanche Indians were a tribe that performed the Sun Dance only once. It varied from other Sun Dances.

The ceremony was sanctioned in visions or dreams by the medicine man Ishatai. The festival was held in mid-summer and lasted eight days; it represented birth, life, death and rebirth in the universe. The first four days was for gathering materials. The last four days was for dancing and celebration; four is a division of eight and a perfect number among the Indians. The Sun Dance was held long ago.

Adobe Walls, in the Texas panhandle was an abandoned fort the buffalo hunters led by Colonel Ranald McKenzie, a famous Indian fighter, used as their headquarters and rendezvous. Quanah asked the chiefs of the Arapaho, Kiowa and Southern Cheyenne tribes to smoke the pipe to war on the whites and avenge the death of a friend at the hands of the troops and their Tonkawa scouts. At the same time he was tired of the white-eyes that had killed off the bison for the hides and tongues, leaving the meat to rot. Chief Quanah spoke to his warriors of the waste and they decided to avenge the wrongs. He felt it best to go on a night raid and stage a surprise attack on the buffalo hunters. The Comanche Chief met with all of the allied tribes in the immediate area and asked for their support on the war trail against the whites.

The Comanche medicine man, *Ishatai* told them that the war party would conquer and that his magic would bring back the buffalo. Ishatai described war-paint that would stop the white man's bullets and claimed that Indian horses painted with his magic yellow paint were protected from arrows and bullets. Quanah took old Ishatai along on the raid to provide magical powers.

Chief Quanah led the Quahadi band on the war trail in Texas while Arapaho, Cheyenne, Comanche and Kiowa Indian raiders attacked white settlements from Kansas to the New Mexico region.

In 1874, the Comanche went on the warpath in Texas. The long battle that ensued was called the 1874-1875 Red River Wars in the Texas Panhandle between the U.S. Army and the Southern Arapaho, Comanche, Kiowa, and Southern Cheyenne Indians. The citizenry demanded that the Army restore the peace.

So on June 27, 1874, Chief Quanah Parker formed his war party of allied tribes of some 700 Arapaho, Cheyenne, Comanche and Kiowa braves and rode to Adobe Walls to attack the "white-eyes" buffalo hunters, a mile from the ruins of the original Adobe Walls site. Kiowa Chiefs Lone Wolf and Woman's Heart and their warriors followed Quanah to fight the buffalo hunters at Adobe Walls. Peace-Chief Kicking Bird kept nearly half of the Kiowa from going to war.

Chief Quanah and two of his wives with their hands
over the unborn as protection from paleface's magic.
Photo Courtesy of Footnote.com

Quanah led the massive war party, as they swarmed down on Adobe Walls with only twenty three buffalo hunters, holed up in the fort. The sound was deafening as the thunder of hoof-beats, rifle cracks and war whoops filled the air; 700 warriors attacked the fort. About 100 yards from the fort on the first charge, a bullet from a buffalo hunter's long-rifle shot Chief Quanah's horse out from under him; the second bullet hit the Chief. The Indians' carbine rifles were no match against the buffalo hunter's sharps rifles and the attack was short lived and a loss.

During the battle, a bullet from a plainsman's long-rifle struck Ishatai's horse right between the eyes, killing it. His magic yellow paint did not protect his mount from the sniper's bullet. He claimed that his medicine left because the warriors had killed a skunk, which he forewarned was taboo. Nevertheless, Ishatai lost all credence with his band and had spoken with a forked tongue. The shaman's magic did not help them and they lost all faith in him.

With nine Indians slain and only four buffalo hunters dead, the warriors retreated. A 700 warrior army could have easily wiped out the white-men with a frontal attack, but the Indians did not like the close quarters. Nine warriors were killed and only four hunters. The fight was named "The Second Battle of Adobe Walls." Some believed it should have been named "The Buffalo Wars," since the Comanche fought over government laws passed to exterminate the buffalo.

In the autumn of 1874, Colonel Ranald Mackenzie led the 4th Cavalry to defeat the warring Comanche Indians in Palo Duro Canyon, in the Texas panhandle. They killed only four Comanche braves, but destroyed their blankets, jerky and supplies.

Troops captured and killed 1,400 of the Indians' horses, burning their lodges. Chief Quanah and the Comanche warriors escaped with their lives. They saw the smoke from their burning teepees rise in the sky as they retreated. Mackenzie dealt a deadly blow to the Comanche braves. Now their fighting days were numbered. They were defeated and doomed to leave the plains.

Battle of Palo Duro Canyon fought
during the Red River War of 1874
with the Comanche and the Army
Photo Courtesy of Wikipeda.org

The last siege on the High Plains was in 1875. The Comanche were familiar with Colonel Ranald Mackenzie, who operated from Fort Sill. He ordered the Indians to come in to the fort unconditionally and the band of starving Comanche straggled in to Fort Sill on a hot summer day in June 1875. When the majority of the Comanche surrendered at Fort Sill, Oklahoma, Chief Quanah was not among them. He retreated deeper into the frontier and managed to survive the harsh winter.

Quanah's band of Comanche Indians surrendered and agreed to dwell on the reservation. The buffalo were nearly gone; the beaver were trapped out and their weapons were confiscated. The Army shot all their horses and life as they had known it had passed. The reign of the "Lords of the Southern Plains" was no more. It was the end of an era for them.

Quanah Parker finally came in to Fort Sill, after signing the Treaty of Medicine Lodge and surrendered in 1875, after leading the last band of Comanche Indians on the plains. On June 2, 1875, Quanah and his Antelope band of Comanche Indians were the last to relent and entered Fort Sill. Chief Quanah and 400 Comanche were last to relent and entered Fort Sill, driving 1500 head of horses onto the reservation.

On the reservation, Quanah switched hats and proved to be an excellent financier and politician in the white man's world. He sold grazing rights on the three million acre reserve with leasing fees going to his people from cattle barons.

Quanah was a peaceable chief and was treated with respect by the Army. He had fought bravely to save his people. Quanah transitioned to civilized life quite well. He became a wealthy rancher on the reservation and never forgot his people. Quanah pushed for their education. He promoted leasing of surplus reservation land for raising stock of confederated tribes.

The Chief was appointed Judge of Indian Affairs in 1886. The white men attempted to get the Comanche to divide their reservation into allotments and then sell to them. Quanah Parker traveled to Washington D.C. to change that policy. Indian agents tried to control the Comanche people by gifting and praising them and punished leaders that refused to do the agents wishes.

Comanche War Chief Quanah Parker
Shown with One of his Wives
at Fort Sill in 1905

The Native American Church movement was founded by Quanah Parker about 1890 among the Comanche Indians and spread to other tribes. Members used peyote (hallucinogenic cactus buttons) in their divination. Quanah Parker promoted the church and taught his people the "peyote road" leading the Indians to Jesus Christ, through visions. The sacrament of the shaman was to eat the peyote cactus button raw, portraying wolves eating the heart of the deer (creator).

The shaman identified diseases for healing purposes. The Native American Church was incorporated in Oklahoma in 1918, a non-profit organization, as "the Native American Church," but the Navajo Tribal Council declared the church illegal in 1940 and believed it harmful to Navajo Christians and their culture. The church continued underground until 1967, when it reversed its identification. Membership grew to 50,000, in America, Canada and Mexico by 1966.

The Spanish-American War was fought in 1898. America won and signed the treaty. In 1907, Oklahoma joined the union and the tribes-people in Indian Territory lost their independence, becoming citizens of Oklahoma.

Quanah established the "Comanche Whitehouse," a 12 room residence near Fort Sill, Oklahoma helped by his friend, cattle baron Burke Burnett. He occasionally wore business suits and was a celebrity. He appeared in Teddy Roosevelt's Inaugural parade in 1905.

Quanah died on February 21, 1911, at the age of 64, under the care of a Comanche medicine man in Cache, Oklahoma and was buried beside his mother, Cynthia Ann Parker, whose body had been reinterred there. Two of his wives survived him. In his lifetime, Quanah claimed eight wives and 25 children, a true Comanche.

He has been called the "Last Comanche Chief" and was the most influential Comanche chief ever, the son of an English American mother and a Comanche Indian father. Quanah was considered to be the greatest Comanche War-chief. Descendants of both white and Indian Parkers keep in touch and have family reunions. Quanah, Texas was named for him. Comanche Indians had fought the white man during the Texas-Indian Wars, since 1840 and had resisted the white Eyes' advance for years.

Comanche War Chief Quanah
Photo Courtesy of Wikipedia.org

Map of Comanche Territory
Photo Courtesy of Wikipedia.org

Quanah Parker, Originator of the Native American Church
Photo Public Domain

CHAPTER FIVE
THE PAIUTE WARS

Paiute dwellers at Pyramid Lake were referred to as the Cui Ui Ticutta in their language or "the Sucker fish eaters" and ate Lahontan trout. Paiute Indians were hunters and gatherers. They hunted antelope, beaver, cougar, deer, ducks, fish, fox, geese, and wild turkey. Animals were hunted, trapped and caught in corrals using communal hunts

Chief Winnemucca was the great chief of the entire Northern Paiute Nation. Winnemucca was called "The Giver." He was a generous Chief. He cared for his tribe. Winnemucca made sure that his people had enough food to eat, were well dressed and had fine teepees.

There is a folk story about old Chief Winnemucca. The aging chief was seen by trappers along the Humboldt River. He was wearing only one moccasin. His people began to call him "One Moccasin." In the Paiute language winni was translated, (one) and mucca means (moccasin), or Winnemucca. Once, he came into town wearing little or nothing. Old Chief Winnemucca was given a blue army officers' uniform with brass buttons and hat, which he liked and wore.

Chief Winnemucca II born around 1820 was the son of Old Winnemucca. He was commonly known as Poito or Numaga. Winnemucca was chief, like his father, of the entire Northern Paiute Indian Nation. This included the Carson, Humboldt and Walker River Paiutes. He was less trusting of the whites than his father, Chief Winnemucca. There were about 6,000 Paiute Indians in the mid 1800's in Nevada Territory.

In 1841 Colonel John Bartleson and John Bidwell led an emigrant party wagon-train from St. Louis heading to Fort Hall, southwest through Snake Country along the Humboldt River, through what is present day Nevada, over the mountains into California. The emigrant party told strange tales about a band of curious Snake Indians who followed them, but never attacked them.

Sarah Winnemucca, the chief's granddaughter, told a humorous tale of her grandfather going out to meet the first white men in his territory. When they appeared in the region that is now Nevada, they were the first whites the Paiute had ever seen. Indians came to old Chief

Old Chief Winnemucca,
In the Paiute language winnemucca meant, "One Moccasin."
Photo Courtesy of the Nevada Historical Society

Sarah Winnemucca was the daughter of a Northern Paiute Indian chief in western Nevada and a champion of her people in the Bannock War. Sarah was made honorary chief of the Northern Paiutes. (Courtesy of the Nevada State Historical Society)

Winnemucca and told him of white men with beards that made camp in their vicinity.

Winnemucca had a dream. He had seen white strangers unlike his people coming from the East. Winnemucca was happy and cried out with joy, "They are my white brothers. I knew you would come." You are my white brothers of my dream." The old chief and his trusted sub-chiefs rode out to their camp, expecting to greet them.

When the party of Paiutes arrived, the Euro-Americans were fearful and halted them. With no interpreter, they used hand motions. There was no real communication. Chief Winnemucca acted out and threw down his robes demonstrating that he was unarmed and meant no harm. Still, the white men prevented their advance. Winnemucca was disappointed that they did not greet him but continued to follow. Each night as they camped, the Paiute camped near them, escorting the party for several days. The chief had been so anxious to meet them. Finally, they turned back and returned to their lodges. As the wagons rolled out of sight the emigrants thought they escaped with their lives. Winnemucca returned home, saddened by the whole affair. This most likely was the Bartleson & Bidwell emigrant party, described earlier.

The next company of white people passing through to California was larger than the previous group. John C. Freemont, the American pathfinder, was among the party. Freemont and Winnemucca hit it off. When Lieutenant John Fremont met the old chief, it became a comedy of errors. Lt. Freemont asked "Old Winnemucca" a question. He would answer, "truckee, truckee," which in the Paiute language meant, "all right." Freemont assumed that his name was Truckee and recorded it that way. The name stuck and old Chief Winnemucca became known as Chief Truckee and Captain Truckee.

Winnemucca scouted for Freemont during the Mexican War and fought for Gen. John C. Freemont against Mexican control of California during the mid-1840s. Captain Truckee later accompanied a party of white men traveling over the mountains to California Territory in 1844.

Truckee welcomed the white settlers and served as a guide for various parties crossing the Sierra Nevada. When Sarah was six years

Paiute Warrior
Photo Courtesy of Azusa Publishing, LLC

old, he took her and her mother and sister to California, where she was introduction to white people and the white culture.

Later Sarah learned English when she and her sister stayed with a white family in Mormon Station (now Genoa), Nevada and she also briefly attended a convent school in San Jose, Calif. By the time she was a teenager, Sarah could speak English and Spanish and several Indian dialects.

Some emigrants were so paranoid of Indians that they would shoot them on sight, which caused the Paiutes to fear the pioneers traveling west. Settlers moved onto the land. During the great "California Gold Rush of 1849," prospectors encroached on Paiute lands. In 1859, silver was discovered in Nevada Territory and Paiute woes increased. Prospectors in Silver City, Gold City and Virginia City all had strikes. Thousands of miners moved into the area.

In order to build mine shacks they cut down the Paiute's pinion pines the Paiute people harvested annually for the much needed pine nuts. Their mules grazed on grasses, the seeds normally eaten by the Indians. Cyanide from the silver mines leaked into their streams, killing the fish. The white man drove the game off. Miners stole Paiute's horses. The Indians countered, stealing back cows and horses. Paiutes were forced work in town to live. Because of limited resources in the desert lands, tensions escalated between the Natives and the white man.

Wavoca, a Paiute holy man, had a vision in 1856 of immortal warriors in Ghost shirts dancing in a circle, invincible to white man's bullets as part of "The Ghost Shirt Religion." The frenzy spread, influencing hundreds of Indians to fight the palefaces with hope of redemption.

The surge of hundreds of miners, settlers and ranchers entering the region amassing on Northern Paiute Indian lands in Nevada Territory disturbed the ecology. Palefaces had an adverse effect on the Indians indigenous to the vicinity. The white man came and shot their game. Their cattle ate the seeds and grasses available for food. Their herds trampled the grasses and bushes used for fee by the wildlife. The palefaces stole the Indians' livestock.

The Paiute War of 1860 was provoked by an evil Indian Agent, who held back food, money and seed from the Paiutes. He shorted the Indians of rations at Fort McDermott and Pyramid Lake for some time. The harsh winter of 1859-1860 left the Paiute Indians starving.

A Comstock Lode of silver was discovered by prospectors near Carson City in Nevada Territory. Thousands of miners flocked to that region during the boom. There was a massive influx of Euro-Americans onto Paiute lands. By the spring of 1860, the amount of white men clamoring to the silver fields equaled the total Paiute Indian population in Nevada Territory. The Paiute Indians were becoming more and more agitated. Two Paiute maidens picking pinion nuts were kidnapped. Natchez and other Paiutes scoured the countryside. They found the two girls bound and gagged in a cellar near Carson City; they had been raped by men from Williams Station. The event sparked a Paiute uprising. Indians were agitated and ready to go to war.

On May 6, 1860, a band of Paiutes attacked Williams Station, the general store, saloon, and stage-stop on the Carson River located at the present day Lahontan Reservoir, where the young women had been held. The frenzied braves massacred the occupants killing five men by torching the station with them inside igniting the Paiute War. One man killed was John Fleming, who suffered the fate of his brothers. Another man got away and made it to Virginia City. The attack on Williams Station frightened the citizens causing a panic and a call for help.

A militia was quickly assembled under Major William Ormsby of the Carson City Rangers to apprehend the perpetrators. They were formed of volunteers from Carson City, Genoa, Silver City and Virginia City. They were poorly armed, mounted, and unorganized. They met at William Station and proceeded toward Pyramid Lake.

Army Major Ormsby and more than 100 men searched for the Paiute band in order to punish them, following their tracks along the Truckee River for about 100 miles. The First Battle of the Paiute War between the Paiute, Bannock, and Shoshoni Indians and the white volunteers was fought on May 13, 1860. Young Winnemucca (Numaga) led a war party of Paiute braves to fight the militia on the banks of the Truckee River in a meadow near Pyramid Lake (now Nevada).

The Paiutes used the decoy method, an old Indian trick, a favorite of the Sioux Indians. They sent out a few decoys. A small party of Indians sat on their horses on a bluff and then acted like they were fearful and rode away. The Paiutes fled after being fired upon and then returned fire. The Paiutes continued firing and raced into a ravine. The militia rode after the fleeing decoys into the ravine; they were trapped. The Indians ambushed them; Numaga's braves blocked their retreat.

Suddenly, War Chief Winnemucca and his 600 warriors rode to the south end of the field forming a semi-circle on a low hill. The Paiute warriors surrounded them and began firing on the volunteers from all sides. The fighting escalated. Natchez Winnemucca saw that Major Ormsby was in trouble and rode to help his friend, but it was too late. A brave rode in and shot his friend before he could reach him. Some of the volunteers fled to a grove of trees. Others rode hard pursued by Indians as far as 20 miles. Seventy five of the 105 men were killed and many injured. Only twenty five Paiutes were killed.

Armed conflict was a result of ill feelings for miners and settlers in the Carson River Valley of the Great Basin. Emigrants passed over the Carson Branch of the California Trail and passed by two trading posts, Buckland and Williams Station. Posts handled Central Overland Mail and the Pony Express Riders that supplied the emigrants and mines.

In late June of 1860, Stewart and Hays retraced the path of Major Ormsby's command and met Chief Numaga on the same field as the first battle northeast of Pyramid Lake. Eight hundred Federal troops and parts of the California Militia were dispatched to the vicinity.

The Second Battle of Pyramid Lake near Truckee River took place in response to the defeat of the U.S. Militia at the First Battle of Pyramid Lake. On June 2, 1860, the well organized force of militia and regulars, the Washoe Regiment, under the capable leadership of legendary Texas Ranger Colonel John C. (Jack) Hayes formed. Hays and his regiment of 500 volunteers defeated several hundred Northern Paiute warriors led by Chief Numaga. This time, the Paiute were outnumbered and retreated into the mountains. After two hours, the battle was over. The warriors fell back to rejoin their families in safety.

Paiute Horsemen 1873
Photo Public Domain

A cease fire was agreed in August of 1860. Within months, a treaty was written. One minor skirmish occurred before the Paiutes disbanded across the Great Basin. After the Second Battle of Pyramid Lake Stewart's regulars hung around for a while before moving into the Carson Sink near Williams Station on the Carson River in order to construct Fort Churchill to defend the citizenry. Fort Churchill was established in 1860 to protect the Pony Express Riders and settlers. Land was designated at Pyramid Lake for a reservation.

Col. Frederick Lander set up a meeting with Numaga. The Colonel promised them the Pyramid Lake Reservation and that they would be taught to farm. Winnemucca was in agreement, but the Army reneged. Reserve land was leased to ranchers. Supplies came late and the Indian agent stole the shipments. He started his own store and sold the food and clothing back to the Indians, making them pay for their own supplies. No one taught them to farm and because of the conditions, they left the reservation. Many faced starvation and died, including Winnemucca's wife. Some worked in town. Others fished and hunted. Some looted as repayment for their treatment.

Owens Valley, California is one of more than 150 desert basins that form the Great Basin region in the western United States. Owens is a narrow valley that lies north by northwest and is bounded by the Sierra Mountains on the west and the White and Inyo Mountains on the east. It extends northward from the Coso Range south of Owens Lake for over 100 miles to the bend in the Owens River north of the town of Bishop, California.

The Owens River Valley Paiutes lived in bands in close proximity. Owens Valley was the home of the Northern Paiute Indians for centuries. The Paiutes spoke the Uto-Aztecan language. They were farmers, hunters and root gatherers. An important food source was the pinion pine-nut. They also gathered hyacinth and yellow nut tubers. The flies laid their eggs on the surface of the saline Owens Lake and the Paiutes used the larvae as a food source. Owens Valley Paiute Indians also hunted big-horn sheep, deer, fish and small game. They built elaborate irrigation ditches to flood their crops of wild hyacinth and yellow nut-grass.

Joseph Reddeford Walker had been the first white man to visit Owens Valley in 1833. John C. Freemont traveled through later and named the Owens Lake for Richard L. Owns. The Owens River and Valley took their name from the lake. Owens Valley was a popular thoroughfare to the Nevada mining districts, the Great Salt Lake and Southern California. Owens Valley became an important military route.

In 1859, US Army Captain John W. Davidson led Companies B and K, 1st Dragoons in search of cattle presumed stolen by the Paiute Indians from ranches in San Fernando and Santa Clara Valleys. Instead, Davidson found a peaceful industrious people that he believed warranted protection, so he recommended that a reservation be set aside for them there free of white settlement and promised the Indians the same. Congress however disagreed and did not believe that the valley could support 30-60 thousand Indians and recommended relocation.

Gold and silver discoveries in the mountains east of the Sierra Mountains drew thousands of prospectors to the region. Then in 1859, L.R. Ketcham of Visalia, California made the first cattle drive through Owens Valley.

In 1861, Allen Van Fleet drove cattle from Carson Valley, Nevada and built a cabin on the Owens River northeast of present day Bishop, California. At the same time, the McGee and the Summer family drove cattle from the San Joaquin Valley into the Owens Valley. The McGee bunch wintered on Lone Pine Creek.

Charles Putnam, part of the McGee outfit, built a trading post using stone north of Lone Pine Creek at Little Pine. Samuel Bishop also brought hundreds cattle and 50 horses from Fort Tejon to Owens Valley in 1861.

The winter of 1861-1862 was one of the harshest in the history of Owens Valley leaving the plight of the Paiutes in bad shape. During the winter blight little game remained, died or was run off. The Paiutes were starving. The cattle were eating the Indians' yellow nut-grass and wild hyacinth.

The Owens Valley Indian War of 1861-1863 was one of many campaigns conducted out West by the Second Cavalry California Volunteers at the time of the Civil War. The Paiutes were used to killing

Paiute Band 1873
Photo Public Domain

game; killing cattle did not seem too different. The cattle had been grazing on Indian land anyway. Then, Al Thompson caught an Indian red-handed butchering a steer; he shot and killed him. The Indians went on the war path. A Paiute war party on the rampage captured a man named Yank Crossen, who was traveling from Nevada to Southern California. White men began to arm themselves and tensions ran high.

In February of 1862, Jesse Summers rode south from Aurora, Nevada to purchase some cattle from the McGee brothers in Lone Pine. Summers agreed on a price and the McGees began to drive the cows. Chief Joaquin Jim stopped their progress. The McGees abandoned their cattle and high-tailed-it back to Putnam's Trading Post for help and then rode to the San Francis Ranch, where they encountered Joaquin Jim and his Paiute band. The men spent the night at the ranch and woke to find the Indians had gone and left the cattle. The next morning the ranchers herded the cattle toward Aurora, Nevada, but lost 200 cows that night to rustlers and turned the herd south through Owens Valley.

Shortly thereafter, a group of cattlemen, including Van Fleet, saw four Paiute Indians in hot pursuit of some stray cows. After confronting the braves, the Indians made up some story about searching for their horses. A fight broke out, resulting in the death of the four braves. Van Fleet and Tom Hubbard were wounded. One of the Paiutes killed was Chief Shondow, a popular leader. His death caused other Paiutes to go on the war path.

Owens Valley ranchers became alarmed. They banned together at Putnam's Trading Post fully armed and rightly so. A band of hostile Paiutes attacked a cabin near Benton Hot Springs. E.S. Taylor, a local prospector, defended his cabin from Indians for two days and killed ten Indians. Then, when the Indians torched his cabin, Taylor was forced out and killed.

On March 20, 1862, Owens Valley settlers decided to raid an Indian encampment in the Ambama Hills, just north of Lake Owens. The Paiutes were poorly armed and easily overpowered. Eleven Indians were slaughtered in the massacre and a ton of meat was destroyed. Three settlers were wounded. The Paiutes sent word to their Northern Paiute allies at Pyramid Lake, but they had recently been defeated in the Paiute

War of 1860. The chiefs warned the bands about participating in the Owens Valley War.

The business of Wingate and Chon in Aurora, Nevada sold guns and ammunition to the Indians because they thought the Paiutes were treated wrongly in cattle deals by the settlers in Owens Valley, but they refused to sell arms to the settlers. The settlers panicked and contacted the Army in Los Angeles and Fort Tejon.

On March 17, Colonel James H. Carleton received correspondence from Mr. Bishop of Owens Valley and Colonel W.A. Bowie from Fort Tejon requesting military assistance due to the Indian uprising. Colonel Bowie immediately issued special orders for Lieutenant Colonel George S. Evan, Second Cavalry, California Volunteers to proceed to Owens Valley via Fort Tejon including Cavalry Companies G, I, and K at Camp Latham. Colonel Evan reported back to military authorities from Owens Valley. The party took 40 days rations and 100 rounds of ammunition per man.

Ranchers moved their herds about 30 miles north of Owens Lake and sent messages to Aurora, Nevada and Visalia, California asking for help for fear of Indian attack. March 28, 1862, eighteen volunteers under John L. Kellogg, a former Army captain, arrived from Aurora. Twenty two men led by Colonel Mayfield came from Visalia and marched 50 miles north up the valley.

Lieutenant Colonel Evan and his Cavalry detachment arrived at Owens Lake on April 2, 1862; they reached Putnam's fort on the 4th of April. They discovered the fort under siege by a war party. The nearly 30 Paiute braves retreated at the sight of the Cavalry. Colonel Evan left seven men to guard the supplies and started up the valley with the remainder of the men.

Indian Agent Colonel Warren Wasson had contacted James W. Nye, Governor of Nevada, concerning a peace mission to Owens River Valley in order to prevent war from spreading across Nevada Territory. Governor Nye approved the mission and contacted General Wright, Department of the Pacific to send a 50 man detachment. Wright ordered Captain E.A. Rowe, Commander of Company A, 2nd Cavalry, California Volunteers and Post Commander, Fort Churchill, Nevada to provide the necessary men. Rowe ordered Post Lieutenant Herman Noble, 2nd Cavalry in Aurora, Nevada, to proceed with Colonel Wasson to Owens Valley on a peacekeeping mission. They met on April 4th, about 30 miles south of Aurora and rode on to Owens Valley.

April 5th, about 500 Paiute mounted warriors appeared near the mountains southwest of Mayfield's party. The Cavalry split in two and attacked the Indians. One white man, C.J. Putnam was killed. The soldiers panicked and retreated. The Paiutes followed and the men had to take refuge in an irrigation ditch for cover through the night.

The sheriff of Mono County, N. F. Scott, was killed by Indians when he lit his pipe at night. The white men retreated under cover of darkness, yet three men died. They made their escape during the night, losing all of their horses and supplies.

On April 6th, Colonel Evans met the citizen soldiers retreating toward Putnam's Fort. Both groups bivouacked for the night about 30 miles north of the fort, at Big Pine Creek. They found two bodies there, killed by Indians. The bodies were Hansen and Talman of Aurora, Nevada.

On April 7th, Colonel Evans was ready to march. Colonel Mayfield joined him with 40 men ready to fight the Indians. As they moved north, Colonel Evans saw some movement some three miles to the east and sent Lieutenant French and five men to investigate. It turned out to be Lieutenant Noble and 50 men from Fort Churchill on their way south to Putnam's Fort. Colonel Evans halted his command until Lieutenant Noble and his men caught up and then proceeded to the battle ground, where no Indians were found.

On April 8th, three parties of scouts embarked to look for Indians. The scouts returned to report seeing a large band of Indians twelve miles away near Bishop Creek, but the Indians scattered at the approach of the Cavalry. The soldiers moved through a blinding snowstorm to reach them, but found no Indians. Colonel Evans sent a patrol of nine men from Company A, on April 9th to investigate the canyon, where campfires had been observed the night before.

On April 10th, 1862, Colonel Evans' command was completely out of provisions, after feeding the citizens of Owens Valley and his

,men. Evans decided to return some 400 miles to Camp Latham for supplies accompanied by Lieutenant Noble and his detachment, via Fort Putnam.

Owens Valley settlers demanded protection from Colonel Evans, who explained to them that he had no authority to leave government troops for their protection or no provision to leave with them. They were given three choices: they were given the prerogative to remain in the valley, accompanied by Colonel Evans, or leave the valley. The settlers chose to leave and drive to their cattle, which consisted of 4,000 cows and 2,500 sheep out of the valley.

On April 14th, Colonel Stevens began the long trip back to Los Angeles and Lieutenant Noble returned to Aurora, Nevada. On April 28th, Colonel Evans arrived at Camp Latham and recommended that a fort be established in Owens Valley for the protection of the citizens there and the route to the Nevada mines, except Placerville. On May 2nd, 1862, General Wright ordered two or three companies of men of the Second Cavalry under the command of Lieutenant Colonel G.S. Evans to establish a military fort in Owens Valley.

On June 14th, 1862, Colonel Evans and 200 men of companies D, G, and I of the Second Cavalry of California Volunteers left Camp Latham for Owens Valley. A train of 46 wagons transported the equipment, ammunition, and rations for the soldiers for 18 days. The Cavalry chased the Paiute Indians for five days; Colonel Evans decided that the warriors would not dare to fight and that a permanent fort was needed. On July 4th a military camp was established on Independence Day at Oak Creek in Owens Valley and appropriately named Camp Independence.

On July 7th, Captain Rowe, Company A, 2nd Cavalry Volunteers at Camp Independence and Mr. Wasson the Indian Agent, met with the local Paiute Indian chiefs and made a treaty with them. Rowe and Evans orders were conflicting. Captain Rowe was on a peacekeeping mission, while Colonel Evans was instructed to chasten the Indians.

A meeting was arranged between Evans, Rowe and Captain George, Paiute chieftain. Paiute War Chief Captain George spoke and stated that he did not want to fight anymore and wanted to befriend the white man. Colonel Evans believed that many of Wasson's promises could not be kept and said that if the troops were withdrawn, the attacks would resume.

Terms of the Indian treaty were concluded by the Department of the Pacific in San Francisco, that the Indians were to restore all of the property stolen from the white man and surrender five hostages as a token of good faith. Some Indians surrendered themselves and their families as hostages. One of these was Captain George, as war chief, Tinemba and several more

J.H.P. Wentworth, Indian Agent for the Southern California District met with Colonel Wasson and as a result sent a message to the Indians to assemble at Camp Independence. They met and on October 6th a treaty was signed. Most of the troops returned to Camp Latham while Company G, under Captain Goodman stayed on to keep the peace. Captain George was held at Camp Independence to ensure the treaty.

A treaty was held at San Francis Ranch with the U.S. Army and the Northern Paiutes on January 31, 1863. Since an equal number had died, one white man and one Indian, a truce was signed. Paiutes agreed not to steal any more cows if the white man controlled grazing. Although both sides agreed to the peace treaty, one Paiute, Chief Joaquin Jim of the Southern Mono Paiutes refused to sign; he and his band began stealing cattle, which ended the treaty.

Peace continued until March 1st, 1863, when Captain George suddenly vanished. Captain Ropes, the new camp commander sent word to the settlement to be on their guard against Indian attack. Several mines and ranchers were killed over the following days. Captain Robes sent word to Camp Babbit requesting help. Camp Babbit immediately sent First Lieutenant S.R. Davis with 44 men to reinforce Camp Independence.

On March 11, 1863, Lieutenant Dougherty led a small patrol of six troops to the Black Rocks and encountered a band of 200 Paiute Indians. A battle broke out and immediately one soldier was killed and four more were wounded, including Dougherty. Three days later, Ropes led 27 men and several civilians out to find the Indians, but could not locate them.

On March 19, a settler described witnessing 30 or 40 Indian rustlers slaughtering cattle eleven miles south of Camp Independence in the Alabama Hills. The Indians scattered and a chase followed. Thirty five Indians were killed and the Army had only one man wounded.

On April 4th, Company E, 2nd Cavalry arrived as reinforcements under the Command of Captain Herman Noble. With two full companies in camp, Captain Ropes on April 9th led 120 men and 36 civilians to scout for Indians. The unit located a band of 200 Indians north of Big Pine Creek. The troops had two casualties and the Indians none.

In late April, Captain Moses arrived at Camp Independence as the new camp commander with parts of Company D, 2nd Cavalry, California Volunteers. The Indians were starving, their food caches had been destroyed by the soldiers. On May 22, Captain George rode into Camp Independence to parley and indicated that he wanted peace for his people. As a result, 400 Paiute people came in and laid down their arms. On July 22nd, 900 Paiute Indians were escorted to the reservation ending the Owens Valley Paiute Indian War, with the exception of Captain Joaquin Jim, who resumed raids in 1864, until December of 1864, when he and his the majority of his band were pursued and killed.

The Owens Valley Indian War lasted over two years. The outbreak was caused by Indians desperate for food. Settlers and miners shot the game which the Indians usually ate. They destroyed the pine groves, the Indian's source of pinion pine nuts. Their horses and cattle ate the yellow nut-grass and hyacinth tubers that the Indians normally consumed. The Indians were starving, their food caches had been purposefully destroyed by the soldiers. The Paiute did not have much choice except to go on the war path. It was estimated that around 60 white men and 200 Paiute Indians died in the conflict. Loss of food and mishandling of weapons was their demise.

In May of 1863, Winnemucca promised Nevada Indian Agent John Burche that he would intercede and persuade Chief Pashego (Passe-quah) and the Bannock of Nevada and Idaho to attend a conference. Burche met with the chiefs on the Humboldt River and Pashego promised no more attacks on the palefaces. To insure peace, the chief promised to keep his Bannock away from major routes and agreed, if the white man left the Indian alone.

In 1865, Chief Winnemucca and men from his Paiute band were on a fishing trip; the Nevada Volunteer Cavalry came and massacred 32 old men, women and children. Winnemucca's youngest son was killed and his two wives were murdered. One wife was the mother of Sarah and Natchez. Sarah hastily rode for her life to safety. Chief Winnemucca took part of his band and departed for Oregon Territory leaving his son, Natchez in charge of the Reservation.

Sac Fox War Chief Black Hawk Painting
By George Catlin
Photo Courtesy of Wikipedia.org

Sketch of Chief Black Hawk
Proponent of the Utah Black Hawk War
Photo Courtesy of Wikipedia

CHAPTER SIX
THE BLACK HAWK WARS

There were two Black Hawk Wars in America. In May of 1832, the Sac and Fox Indians returned to their native lands in northern Illinois led by Black Hawk creating pandemonium among white settlers. The Sac Fox warrior, called Black Hawk was drawn into war to resist the influx of white intruders on their lands. The other Black Hawk War occurred in Utah a few years later.

Ma-ka-tai-me-she-kia-kiah (Black Hawk) was born in 1767 in a village called Saukenuk in present day Illinois. He fought the principal enemy, the Osage Indians, and gained the reputation of a fierce warrior. Black Hawk became chief of his people. At the turn of the century, Black Hawk had turned his anger towards the white settlers that streamed onto Indian lands. The Indians lost their native lands in Illinois in the disputed St. Louis treaty held in 1804. Black Hawk said that the treaty was signed by drunken Indian representatives and refused to accept it. Finally, Black Hawk signed the treaty in 1816, but they continued their raids

A soldier named Abraham Lincoln, who was 23 years of age, was captain in the Illinois militia. Lincoln rejoined the service twice, but never saw action. Abraham Lincoln would go on to become President of the United States. Like most wars, being in the service seems to help men advance in politics. Four Illinois governors served in the Black Hawk War. Jefferson Davis was one who succeeded and became President of the Confederacy.

General Atkinson was the commander during the Black Hawk frontier war, but was replaced for mishandling the conflict allowing it to turn bloody and drag on. It was believed that if Major Isaiah Stillman had been in command, the hostiles would have gone back west of the Mississippi without a shot fired. Atkinson was removed from leadership.

The Illinois militia tried to locate Black Hawk and the evasive band of Sac and Fox Indians. As the U.S. Army built more and more forts, droves of settlers moved onto Indian lands. When the settlers began to occupy the Sac village of Saukenuk, Chief Black Hawk declared war on the white settlers. In April 1832, The Sac Fox and Kickapoo Indians, who returned to Illinois with Black Hawk, joined by

Potawatomi and Winnebago Indians made the war devastating. Many settlers lost their lives during the Indian War and Indians died at the hands of the Army or Militia.

Chief Black Hawk decided to find refuge among the Chippewa Indians. His tribe became tired and discouraged and refused to follow him. The Sac and Fox that had remained west of the Mississippi River disavowed allegiance to Black Hawk and even turned over some of his supporters to the army. They picked up the Indians' trail and began to follow Black Hawk and his band across northern Illinois and southwestern Wisconsin.

On August 1, 1832, Chief Black Hawk returned to the native lands west of the Mississippi River in Iowa. Their attempt to cross the mighty river in handmade canoes or rafts wound up in disaster and several drowned. Some survived. Black Hawk saw an American steamboat, "the Warrior." He knew the captain and waved a white flag. Misunderstanding, the soldiers aboard the ship opened fire on them.

The following morning on August 2, 1832, soldiers reached the Sac and Fox. Soldiers approached the rag-tag group of disbanded Indians, mostly women and children, trying to get to safety. The soldiers opened fire on the Indians. Many managed to escape. Others died crossing the river or were shot by Sioux warriors positioned on the west side of the river. Fifty or sixty Sac-Fox died. Finally, the militia massacred the Sac-Fox at the Battle of Bad-Axe on the Mississippi River, ending the Black Hawk War of 1832. When Black Hawk heard the news, he grieved and turned himself in shortly thereafter.

In late September of 1832, Army General Scott and Illinois Governor Scott Reynolds met with the tribal chiefs just west of Fort Armstrong. Reynolds and Scott initially demanded most of Iowa as indemnity for the war and offered payment of $20,000 annually for the next 30 years. Sac Chief Keokuk insisted that the annuity be increased to an annual payment of $30,000 and a parcel of land to be reserved for the Sac and Fox Indians. They agreed on a settlement and the treaty was successful. General Scott and Governor Reynolds signed a similar treaty with the Winnebago Indians two weeks prior demanding that the Winnebago surrender all of their lands south and east of the Fox and

Wisconsin rivers in Illinois and Wisconsin. In exchange, they received a parcel of land in Iowa between the Sioux and Sac Fox rivers. The Sac Fox had long been mortal enemies of the Sioux. The Winnebago however, remained neutral.

The survivors returned to their villages east of the Mississippi River; most Indians were rounded up and moved to Fort Armstrong on Rock Island. The irony of all this was that there was a cholera outbreak at the fort.

General Scott released most of the Indians so that they would not contract the disease. Eleven Indians were held in custody for seven months. This included chiefs Black Hawk, Napope, White Cloud and five other chiefs of the tribe. Effigies of the prisoners were burned in Detroit by an unruly crowd.

They were escorted by Jefferson Davis on June 5, 1833 and sent by steamboat to Jefferson Barracks in St. Louis and confined. While in confinement, famed artist George Catlin sketched the prisoners only if he depicted them wearing their ball and chains.

∧∧◇∧∧

Sunday April 9, 1865, Ulysses S. Grant and Robert E. Lee sat down at the Appomattox Court House, Virginia and negotiated a conclusion to the Civil War. On the same day, April 9, 1865, a handful of Mormon ranchers found a band of starving Ute Indians near Manti, Utah feasting on the meat of Mormons cows. A drunken Mormon yanked an Indian chieftain off his horse in anger. The insulted Ute Indians rode off promising retaliation. One Indian in the band was another chief called Black Hawk, who also went by Antonga. The inebriated Mormon had unknowingly started the Black Hawk War.

The war in Utah lasted longer than any war in Utah. Tension had been building between settlers and the Indians in Utah for years. Black Hawk returned with an angry Ute Indian war party. The band massacred five Mormons and escaped into the mountains driving hundreds of the Mormons' stolen cattle. Again, starving Indians were found eating Mormon steaks. Soon Black Hawk was promoted to war chief.

The Ute Indians dwelled in the Great Basin for 10,000 years. They were the first American tribe to own horses from the Spanish.

85

From 1865-1867, Uintah Ute Indian Chief Antonga Black Hawk led a band of Ute Indian braves to rustle stock from Mormon ranchers. He was the brother of principle Ute Chief Tabby. That year, Chief Black Hawk and his Navajo, Paiute and Ute Indian war party stole over 2,000 head of cattle and killed 25 whites. The war was heaviest from 1865-67. Black Hawk incited dozens of allies to join them and go on the warpath against the Mormons. Herdsmen, settlers, and travelers were massacred on the trail.

Information about the raids was withheld from the government since Brigham Young and the Mormon Church were at odds with the Federal government so the war was kept a secret. Instead, Brigham Young mobilized a force from the church ranks called the Nauvoo Legion to protect the settlers.

Members of a pioneer family outside of Denver were murdered by Indians on the war path during the Indian Wars (the Cheyenne–Arapaho War or the Colorado War of 1864-65) by Indians.

Another incident near there was caused by Piede Indians. The local Paiute Indians of the Piede band had been pacifistic toward the palefaces, but in late April of 1865, two members of the Piede Paiute band shot and wounded a soldier from Fort Sanford.

The Utah militia promptly stripped the band of their weapons. They were put under guard and held at the court house. Women and children were kept in the cellar. The Indians loosed their bonds and attacked the guards. The guards in turn, shot the Indians. Soon, all of the escapees were dead, so they brought up the women and children and silenced them.

May 26, 1865, Ute Indians raided the John Givens family. Givens, his wife, and son were shot to death. Daughters aged three, five, and nine were bludgeoned to death by Ute tomahawks. That same year, War Chief Black Hawk led a war party that killed five settlers near Ephraim, including two women. Circleville was a new town west of the Sevier River. The residents had little experience fighting Indians. So, when the Ute Indians attacked November 26, 1865, and lives were lost, the townspeople fled in fear to the meetinghouse for safety fighting from there.

James Froid tried to save his cattle. The Indians saw him. He was captured and stripped. They peppered him with arrows and bullets. Hans Christian Hansen and two teen-age boys were murdered. Attacks continued into 1867. Mormon settlers began to desert their homes and built stockade forts, while Mormon militia men chased the illusive Indians through the outback. Requests for federal troops went unheeded for eight years. Not knowing one from the other, Indians were killed in general.

In the fall of 1867, a peace was made, but open warfare continued though it began to diminish. More and more white people came west and upset the harmony of the ecology of the American Indian. The white man brought diseases. They killed off game that the Indians much needed for sustenance and took lands that the Indian had lived on for thousands of years. The government passed laws to have the buffalo removed in order to get the Indians to transition onto reservations.

Another peace treaty was signed in 1868, but the raiding and killing did not stop. Mormon militiamen pursued the war parties, but to no avail. After bloodshed on both sides, much needed troops were ordered in 1872.

When the troops finally arrived, two hundred federal troops emerged to finalize the seven year, Black Hawk War. It was Utah's longest Indian War and caused more destruction than any other war, but finally the fighting was over in 1873. Seventy five settlers were killed in the conflict. The number of deaths among the Ute Indians is not known. Mormons found themselves in open warfare with Black Hawks' Navaho, Paiute and Ute warriors. In all, there were 150 battles during the Black Hawk War, with dozens of skirmishes and scores of deaths.

A treaty was signed between the U.S. government and the Ute Indians in 1873. The Ute Indian Reservation was established in 1863. The Unitah Ute Indians transitioned to the Indian reservation at fort Duchesne, Utah in 1864. The Unitah and Ouray Ute Indian Reservation is the second largest Indian reservation in the United States. The Ute Reservation is 4,500,000 acres. Land surface is 1.2 million acres. Mineral owned land is 40,000 acres.

Sioux Chief Hollow Horn Bear
Photo Courtesy of Wikipedia.org

CHAPTER SEVEN
THE GREAT SIOUX WAR

Sioux Indians were Algonquin speakers of Northern Canada, who expanded into Montana and the Dakotas. They were a warring tribe and fought over territory. The Sioux were enemies of the Shoshoni, also the Blackfoot, Crow, Sac-Fox and Ute. The name Sioux came from a Chippewa word for "Little Snake."

A young Sioux Indian experienced his vision quest. In a revelation, the young brave rode a horse whose hooves did not touch the ground. The horse floated as it galloped and changed colors as did the attire of his rider. The Indian rode effortlessly, seeing grass, sky and trees. He was "Crazy Horse," named for his father.

Crazy Horse had another dream of an incident between Sioux and white man that troubled him. In 1854, a Minnenjou Sioux named "High Forehead" shot a Mormon's cow near the Fort Laramie trading post. Army Lieutenant John Grattan decided to teach the Sioux a lesson. He took 34 soldiers along with two cannons to annihilate the Sioux. Grattan's unit never returned. Later, all 35 men were found massacred.

The Dakota War in Minnesota began the morning of August 18, 1862. War erupted with attacks by the Lower Sioux Indians led by Chiefs Cut Nose and Little Crow. Captain John Marsh rode from Fort Ridgely, Minnesota with a small band of 46 men, who were ambushed by the Sioux.

The next day, Colonel Sibley and 1,169 troops left Fort Ridgely for Wood Lake and camped overnight. At daybreak, soldiers acting against orders took wagons to pick potatoes at the Sioux Agency. The men in the wagons were ambushed by the Sioux. The attack alerted the men in camp. A short skirmish occurred. The Sioux were so outnumbered that they retreated to their encampment.

Colonel Chivington and the Colorado Volunteers ambushed Chief Black Kettle's Cheyenne tribe at the Sand Creek Massacre in 1864 killing women and children. Chief Black Kettle was absent and his life was spared.

In the words of the famous Kit Carson. "Jis to think of that dog Chivington and his dirty hounds, up thar at Sand Creek. His men shot

down squaws, and blew the brains out of little innocent children. You call sich soldiers Christians, do ye? And Indians savages? What der yer 'spose our Heavenly Father, who made both them and us, thinks of these things? I tell you what, I don't like a hostile red skin any more than you do. And when they are hostile, I've fought 'em, hard as any man. But I never yet drew a bead on a squaw or papoose, and I despise the man who would."
Kit Carson

In 1865, 1866 and 1868, the U.S. Government wrote treaties with the Sioux Nation. In the treaty of 1868 the Great Sioux Reservation was born. Later, in 1875 the Red Cloud Delegation visited President Grant in Washington D.C. Chiefs Red Cloud, Sitting Bull, Spotted Tail, and Swift Bear of the Sioux Nation attended. They met with the President of the United States about the purchase of the Black Hills.

In 1873, the Battle of Massacre Canyon occurred in southwestern Nebraska, when several tribes were off the reservation simultaneously for their annual buffalo hunt. The Pawnee Indians were accompanied by an Indian Agent and had been told that they would have protection against any hostile historical enemy tribes.

Over 1,000 Sioux warriors attacked the Pawnee hunting party at the head of the canyon. The running battle ranged over several miles. The Pawnee became trapped in the lower portion of the canyon near the Republican River. Sixty nine men, women and children were killed, others died later from their wounds. The Sioux claimed six killed.

In 1876, the Sioux Indians were ordered to the Rosebud Reservation or be considered hostiles. General Crook embarked from Fort Walla-Walla to engage the Cheyenne and Sioux. Shoshoni Indians fell in behind Crook's column to give battle to their old enemy. Crook attacked the Indian encampment on Rosebud Creek but met defeat.

Sioux Chief Red Cloud gained respect as a warrior. He waged Red Cloud's War against the soldier forts and miners along the Bozeman Trail, which cut through Sioux hunting grounds. He came in to Fort Laramie and signed the 1868 Peace Treaty, relinquishing the Black Hills. Red Cloud was with the Sioux delegation to Washington D.C. in 1875. He was an important chief orator and statesman for the Sioux Nation.

Great Medicine Man & War Chief Sitting Bull
Photo Courtesy of Azusa Publishing, LLC

The Great Sioux War Chief Red Cloud
Photo Courtesy of Azusa Publishing, LLC

Sioux War Chief Gall
Photograph Courtesy of Azusa Publishing, LLC

Chief Rain-in–the-Face Claimed He Killed Tom Custer
Photograph Courtesy of Azusa Publishing, LLC

Original Photo of Thomas Ward Custer, brother of George
Custer, who fought in his ranks. Tom died at the Little Bighorn
Courtesy of Theron Ludlow

General George Armstrong Custer
Photo Courtesy of Wikipedia.org

Crow Scout "White Man Runs Him"
Photograph Courtesy of Azusa Publishing, LLC

HairyMoccasin
Photo Courtesy of Azusa Publishing Company LLC

Sitting Bull in the Sioux language was called Tantanka Iyotanka. He also had a dream. In his vision he saw soldiers descending onto them like grasshoppers, but the soldiers fell on the ground in defeat.

Lt. Colonel George Custer was transferred out West to lead the 7th Cavalry. He led the attack on the Indians at the Battle of Washita. After he married Elizabeth "Libbie" Bacon, Libbie often dined with George in the field, while his brother, Tom and nephew, Boston rode in his ranks.

Custer had led the attack on the Indians at the Battle of Washita and killed Chief Black Kettle. He was loathed by the Indians and hated by Captain Fredrick Benteen, one of his officers.

Custer's Cavalry had ridden all night in order to reach Rosebud Sioux Indian Village in South Dakota. The overconfident Custer would not take the advice of his Indian scouts and retreat because of the Indians' large numbers.

Hairy Moccasin was a Crow scout who volunteered under Lt. James Bradley's detachment of Indian Scouts. He served as scout for service for the U.S. Army 7th Cavalry under General Gibbons, General Howard, Captain Miles and Lt. Col. Custer.

Hairy Moccasin was reported to have given the size and position of the Sioux encampment at the valley of the Little Bighorn. Headed for disaster, Custer wanted to kill Indians. He was psyched up talking to his scouts. He rode among his troops to bolster them. The general was excited about fighting the battle.

Custer's Arikara and Crow Indian scouts prepared to die, knowing their fate. Yellow Hair (Custer) was in disbelief of the number of Sioux amassed there. An interesting narrative about Custer's Crow scouts is that they changed out of their army uniforms into Indian garb. When questioned by Custer, they explained how they wanted to die in their own tradition. Custer got very angry, swore and dismissed them from duty.

Custer divided his ranks into two, while Major Marcus A. Reno took two companies and Captain Fredrick Benteen led one company of men to southwest Glen Creek, then rode along the east side of the river. Benteen was to stay close and if no Indians were seen, return to ranks.

On June 25, 1876, George Armstrong Custer led five companies of his U.S. Seventh Cavalry in hot pursuit of the Sioux Indians along the Little Bighorn River in Montana Territory. He made a fatal mistake dividing his companies into three groups. The Cheyenne Indians remembered "Long Hair" from his massacre of Chief Black Kettle's village and hated Custer with a passion. Their leader, Sitting Bull had gathered the largest army of Indians ever assembled on the Columbia Plateau. 2,000 Arapaho, Blackfoot, Cheyenne and Sioux Indian warriors under Chiefs Sitting Bull, Crazy Horse, Gall, Red Cloud, and Spotted Tail were ready to attack.

On a hot day in June, Custer's three companies rode hard, charging Sitting Bull's village. Custer and Reno's offensive approached both ends of the Rosebud Sioux village. Sitting Bull's adopted brother, Chief Gall and sub-chief under him, led the attack on the Bluecoats. Major Marcus Reno attacked at the other end of the encampment. Chief Gall routed Major Reno and met Custer's forces head on with hundreds of Sioux warriors for a decisive frontal attack. As General Custer's battalion fought for their lives, Major Reno and Captain Benteen were engaged in the thick of battle. Major Reno was in trouble. Benteen rallied his men and came to his defense. Reno's army, reinforced by Captain Benteen's men had losses but survived to live and fight another day

Custer and his complement were outnumbered and surrounded by the Sioux Cavalry. Two hundred and ten men were massacred by Sioux Indians at "Custer's Last Stand," at the Little Bighorn. Sioux War-chiefs Gall and Crazy Horse were credited with conquering the 7th Cavalry. Custer died in battle on June 25, 1876. A statue of George Armstrong Custer, on his horse was erected near Monroe, Michigan.

Chief American Horse of the Ogallala Sioux was a warrior orator and diplomat to the government for his people. After the tragic Wounded Knee Uprising, he became the leader of the Sioux delegation representing his people to Washington. American Horse was one of the Sioux Chiefs who later performed in Buffalo Bill's Wild West Show.

May 1877, Sitting Bull escaped to Canada about the same time Crazy Horse surrendered at Fort Robinson. That year General Miles defeated a small band of Minnenjou Sioux, ending the Sioux War.

Sketch of Custer's Last Stand
Photo Courtesy of Wikipedia.org

Custer's Scouts at Battlefield
Azusa Publishing Company, LLC

Cheyenne Chiefs Little Wolf & Dull Knife
Courtesy of Azusa Publishing, LLC

Northern Cheyenne Chief Dull Knife (Morning Star) had been an advocate of peace with the white man, who was invading the Powder River Country of modern day Montana and Wyoming. He signed the treaty at Fort Laramie in 1868. The winter of 1877, Dull Knife's band was camped at the headwaters of the Powder River. General Ranald McKenzie led a winter campaign of an expeditionary force to avenge the deaths of the soldiers at the Little Bighorn. In November of 1877, McKenzie's men discovered the village of Dull Knife's Cheyennes. The fight ensued. In the Dull Knife Fight 153 lodges were destroyed and 500 war ponies captured; most of the Cheyenne surrendered. Chief Dull Knife was forced to surrender the next spring. The same year, Cheyenne Indians were allowed to go onto the Tongue River reservation.

In 1877, Dull Knife's band was relocated to Indian Territory in Kansas-Oklahoma. Unable to hunt for food, the Cheyenne were forced to accept government rations, besieged by disease, and hunger. Chief Dull Knife's and one other band left on a forced march to Wyoming. Once a friend to the white man, Chief Dull Knife was now branded a renegade. Army units from forts in the vicinity searched for the Indians and tried unsuccessfully to detain Dull Knife's band, but he outmaneuvered them in the Nebraska Sand Hills.

They arrived in Fort Robinson in Nebraska, near their Wyoming home, where they surrendered to the Army in hopes of returning to their homeland. Instead, they were told to return to Indian Territory in Oklahoma. Unwilling to accept these terms, Chief Dull Knife and 100 of the band fled in the night in a desperate attempt to be free. On January 8, 1878, Soldiers from Fort Robinson massacred 30 Cheyenne men, women, and children. Chief Dull Knife managed to escape and wound up on the Sioux reservation in Nebraska. The Chief died in 1883 and was buried high on a hill at Lame Deer, Montana.

Word about the Ghost Dance in Nevada traveled fast to Fort Hall and into the Plains, reaching the Sioux. In 1890, young Sioux braves did the Ghost Dance in their sacred shirts late one night, giving war-whoops, shooting off rifles and dancing around a huge bonfire at Wounded Knee, South Dakota. The experience frightened nearby settlers. The U.S. Cavalry was called in the next day. Sioux Chief Sitting Bull was pulled from his sleeping robes and shot to death. Sitting Bull's death was the passing of an era.

Many Plains Tribes had surrendered to General Miles in his 1876-77 Campaign. At Pine Ridge Sitting Bull, with the Brule and Oglala Sioux had resisted. After the Ghost Dance in 1890, 300 Sioux Indian Ghost dancers of all ages were killed at "the Great Massacre" at Wounded Knee, South Dakota. Sioux Chief Big Foot surrendered. The Medicine Man's dream had become a nightmare. In 1891, 400 Brule and Ogallala Sioux Indians banded together on the Brule River, known as the Hostile Camp, near Pine Ridge, South Dakota Territory.

The powerful Sioux Indian Nation was a mighty one. They were the only American Indian tribe to defeat the United States Army in battle. The Sioux Indian territory was widespread. The Sioux ranged from Canada across the northern Rock Mountains. They drove smaller tribes from the Black Hills onto the Plains.

Many famous chiefs came from the Sioux tribe: Sitting Bull, Red Cloud, and Crazy Horse were a few. The Sioux tribe had chiefs designated for various aspects of life, war chiefs, local rule, and medicine men, of which Sitting Bull was one. The Sioux were a fierce foe.

The U.S. government feared at the time of the Little Bighorn, that if all of the Indians in the Northwest had united then, they could have wiped out the whole U.S. Army.

Buffalo Bill Cody founded his Buffalo Bill's Wild West show in 1883 in North Platte, Nebraska, taking his large company on tours throughout the United States and, beginning in 1887, in Europe. One of Bill's main attractions was his wild Indians. He preferred to use real live Sioux Indians on horseback for actors. Bill hired famous Sioux Indians to play in his show like Sioux chiefs American Horse, Red Cloud, and Sitting Bull.

Today, there are 30,000 Sioux Indians living in South Dakota. Half of the members live off the reservation in Canada, Montana, and Nebraska. There are five Sioux reservations: Standing Rock Reservation, Cheyenne River Reservation, Lower Brule Reservation, Upper Brule Reservation and Pine Ridge Reservation, all created from the Rosebud Reservation and some smaller reservations.

104

CHAPTER EIGHT
CHIEF JOSEPH &
THE NEZ PERCE WAR

The Nez Perce Indians dwelt in one place in present day northern Idaho, Oregon and Washington for thousands of years and fished in the Snake River region of Hell's Canyon. The heavy rock writing in Hell's Canyon is evidence of their habitation. Hundreds of ancient petro-glyphs appear along the Snake River, on Hell's Canyon's rock and walls. The Nez Perce, Palouse, and Spokane Indians were all sedentary fishermen in the prehistoric days.

At that time, the Nez Perce made up the largest tribe in the Columbia River Plateau, with a population of about 6,000 Native Americans in 300 camps and villages. In 1800, the Nez Perce Country ranged over about seventeen million acres that would become Idaho, Oregon and Washington. The area reached from the Bitterroot Mountains to the Blue Mountain Range.

The Nez Perce called themselves the "Nee-Me-Poo" or "the people." The Nez Perce Tribe in their tongue was "Chutepalu." The Nez Perce spoken language is Nimipuutimpt. Their dialect is from the Plateau Penutian linguistic stock.

Neighboring tribes, the Klamath, Umatilla and Yakima Indians also spoke dialects of the Sahaptian language. Trade was established among Columbia River and Coastal Indians communicating by sign language.

The area teemed with bighorn sheep, bear, cougar, deer and elk which provided good hunting. Salmon runs provided a wealth of fish to eat or store in bundled cakes for winter. The Nez Perce hunted, fished and dug camas bulbs and lived in extended families in villages. Recently archeologists found an ancient fishing village in Hell's Canyon.

It is estimated that the Nez Perce became horse people around 1700. They most probably traded for their first horses and acquired Appaloosa horses from the Comanche Indians or the Shoshoni trade center. The Comanche were the finest horse handlers and horsemen among the Plains Indians.

The Nez Perce and Palouse people are culturally linked. The Palouse spoke their language. The Palouse River was named for the tribe and the countryside around it. Palouse Country evolved from the horse and refers to the fertile, hilly region of Eastern Washington and Northwestern Idaho north of the Snake and Clearwater Rivers. The name, "Appaloosa," for the gorgeous spotted horse came from the Palouse tribe that raised them. They either got the horse from the Comanche, Nez Perce, or the Shoshoni. The name "Palouse," probably came from French fur trappers. The slang word, Appalousey, refers to the horse. The Nez Perce and Palouse both bred and raised the beautiful Appaloosa pony. Over time their herds numbered in the thousands. It was no rare sight to see the Nez Perce trailing 400 mounts to the Shoshoni trade fair.

The Nez Perce were first contacted by the Spanish explorers. Then the Lewis and Clark Expedition arrived in Nez Perce country in 1805 to build additional dugout canoes at a site called "Canoe Camp." Trees were felled along the river for dugout canoes, fashioned from logs. When Lewis and Clark contacted the Nez Perce, they found them scantily dressed. The Indians befriended the men in the Lewis and Clark party. The Nez Perce were civilized and an intelligent race. The men were handsome, six foot in stature and their women fair.

Lewis and Clark first sat down cross-legged on a blanket, smoked the pipe and traded with the Nez Perce in 1805. They told them they did not want red beads, but preferred blue ones. Spanish explorers had earlier brought glass beads for trade with the Indians. They called the pale blue donut shaped bead of the Spanish "a piece of the sky." This was living proof that Spanish conquistadors made contact with the Nez Perce long ago. The explorers, Lewis and Clark heard blue padres called tia com-mo-shack, in the Nez Perce language, meaning "chief of beads."

When the Lewis and Clark party passed through, the Nez Perce agreed to allow passage through their country and never to make war with the white man. The Nez Perce tribe held the party's horses as they crossed the Rocky Mountains, until their return. They found passage through the Rocky Mountains, by canoeing the Clearwater River to the Snake and then on to the Columbia and the Pacific Ocean.

Chief Joseph loved his country and respected his father's wishes. Tuekakas had told him never to give up the land that held his peoples' bones. When he became chief Joseph tried to keep his promise.
Courtesy of Azusa Publishing, LLC

Chief Joseph in Hudson's Bay Blanket
Photo Courtesy of Wikipedia.org

Chief Joseph and His Family in 1880
Photo Courtesy of Wikipedia.org

In 1818, an agreement between America and Great Britain was made where Indian land was shared with whites. The United States Bureau of Indian Affairs was created in 1824.

The Nez Perce Indians traded at the fur forts for beads, guns, horses, knives, metal kettles, tobacco, and woven blankets. When hundreds of trappers, and settlers moved into Nez Perce country, half of the Indian populations died of diseases contracted from the white man.

Old Joseph in his native tongue was called Tuekakas, chief of the Wallam-wat-kin (Wallowa) band. Old Joseph, the Elder was one of the first converts to Christianity at the Lapwai Mission. Reverend Spalding performed the marriage ceremony for Tuekakas and Khapkhaponimi. Tuekakas' father was a Cayuse Indian and his mother a Nez Perce.

Chief Joseph described the first white traders that came to their country. They were Frenchmen, the fur traders, who came laden down with goods to trade the Indian for furs and skins. The French called the American Indians, Nez Perce (the pierced nose people) because they pierced their noses and inserted ringed ornaments through them. Joseph recalled stories of Lewis and Clark, who brought trade goods that his people had not seen before. The Nez Perce gave them a great feast to show their hearts were friendly. The men from Clark's party were kind and talked straight. They gave the Chiefs presents and the Indians lavished gifts on them giving food, shelter and horses.

In 1840, a defender of the people was born to the Nez Perce. His name was In-mut-too-yah-lat-lat in the Chutepula (Nez Perce) tongue, meaning "Thunder-Traveling-over-the-Mountains." His common name was Young Joseph. His father was called Old Chief Joseph. He was of the Wallam-wat-kin band of the Chutepula tribe. As a youth, young Joseph attended the Spalding Mission School, run by Rev. Henry Spalding. He spent several years there before returning to Wallowa in Oregon territory in 1847. His father was quite ill then and Joseph took on duties as peacetime village chief and leader.

Old Joseph (Tuekakas) would not have anything to do with the Soldier Peace Council. He warned Young Joseph not to accept gifts from the white man for they might claim the gifts were trade for their land. He also told his son not to give up the land of their fathers. He did not trust anyone who would buy and sell land. The Indians believed that they could not possess the land, but only manage it.

In 1855, Governor Isaac I. Stevens gathered the regional Indian chiefs for a treaty council and a feast. Steven's treaty was signed by the Cayuse, Nez Perce, Umatilla and the Walla-Walla. Lawyer signed, as did Looking Glass and Tuekakas, who signed reluctantly. Old Joseph carried his Bible and U.S. flag. They agreed to cede in land for a large reservation in Wallowa to coexist. This treaty allowed the Nez Perce to keep most of Wallowa but the government would soon break their treaty.

Ruthless Indian agents demanded the Nez Perce leave their scenic Walla-Walla Valley, teeming with creeks, rivers, and game and the beautiful Wallowa Lake and Mountains, for a Lapwai Reservation.

Chief Looking Glass had earned his name because of the signal mirror he wore on a leather thong around his neck. He was a sub-chief under Young Joseph.

10,000 miners and settlers disregarded the treaty and trespassed on lands of the Nez Perce. Indian agents in 1868 demanded the Nez Perce leave their scenic Walla-Walla Valley that teemed with creeks, rivers and game with the beautiful Wallowa Mountains in the background, for a Lapwai Reservation. Young Joseph and his father fought this idea, but Lawyer signed the treaty. By 1870 Washington pushed to place all Indians on reservations. Some went peaceably, many others rebelled.

Young Chief Joseph was a handsome, stately Nez Perce Indian. He was sage and a peace chief. Joseph was polygamous, however. He and took four wives and fathered nine children. Young Joseph took over as chief in governing his band, as blindness slowly darkened his father's eyesight. Finally, the old chief summoned his son to his bedside. He knew that his death was near. He spoke softly and said, "My son, my body is returning to my mother earth, and my spirit is going very soon to see the Great Spirit Chief. In a few more years the white man will be all around you. They have their eyes on this land. My son, never forget my dying words. This country holds your father's body. Never sell the bones of your father and mother." When Old Joseph died in 1871, Young Joseph expressed his feelings in this poem of his father.

I buried him in the valley
of the winding waters. (Wallowa)
I love that land more
than all the rest of the world.

After his father's death, Young Joseph became chief of the Wallowa Nez Perce. He came to be a great orator, statesman and war-chief. Chief Joseph was known as a noble red man to both Indian and white man. After his father's death, Young Joseph became chief of the Wallowa Nez Perce. He stated that a man who would not defend his father's grave is worse than a wild animal. The Nez Perce had been friendly and also fair to the explorers, the fur trappers and the white settlers, but the winds were changing.

In 1872, Smohalla, a Nez Perce prophet proclaimed that Indians would rise up from the dead and drive the white-eyes out of the land, initiating the Dreamer's Religion.

Many white men were coming. The armies began pushing Indians off of their lands. On June 16, 1873, President Grant reserved land in Wallowa Valley for Chief Joseph and the Nez Perce Indians. They were promised Wallowa, but white settlers were greedy and wanted the fertile ground. In 1875, Wallowa was opened for white settlement.

1876 a commission met with the Nez Perce to offer to move them to their reservation by April 1, 1877. General Oliver O. Howard was placed in command of relocation. He had fought in the Civil War, in Mr. Lincoln's Army and lost his right arm, when a Minnie ball struck it.

When General Oliver O. Howard ordered the Palouse Indians to transition onto the Nez Perce Reservation, they rebelled. Both tribes met with Howard at Fort Lapwai in November of 1876 and again in May of 1877.

The Nez Perce chose Chiefs Toohoolhoolsote and White Bird to represent them. The Palouse Indians chose Husishusis Kute, who remained silent, while Toohoolhoolzote explained how mother earth was sacred. Toohoolhoolsote spoke, "I have heard, a trade between some of these of Indians and the white man concerning their land; but I belong to the land which I came. The earth is my mother."

Nez Perce Indian Village at Lapwai
Photo Public Domain

Howard, the Christian General, disliked the two chiefs and their pagan religion. General Howard ordered the Nez Perce and Palouse to leave their traditional lands and move onto the Nez Perce reservation at Lapwai, Idaho. The Indians ultimately agreed and signed the treaty.

The council meeting at Lapwai began on May 2, 1877. Joseph (the orator), narrated the wrongs to his people and the need for them to be treated fairly. Joseph stated that he did not speak with a "forked tongue." General Howard urged them to go on the reservation. The government had taken Joseph's lands, horses and cattle, giving him many reasons to rebel. General Howard broke his promise to Chief Joseph, and ordered the Nez Perce, with livestock, onto the reservation in 30 days, then reordered the soldiers to round up the Indians. Howard had promised him that they could keep Wallowa Valley, (Winding water in the Nez Perce language), but the army took over their land.

The Nez Perce had been friendly and also fair to the explorers, the fur trappers and to the white settlers. Now, the pendulum was swinging the other way. Too many white men were coming. The white man and his armies were pushing them off their lands. Chiefs Joseph, White Bird and Too-hul-hut-sote held a grand council at Lake Tolo at the head of Rocky Canyon. Some wanted war. The statesman Joseph pleaded for peace but was accused of cowardice. Some expected military intervention. In Rocky Canyon they held festivities with dancing, stick games, horse races and parades. They took advantage of their dwindling freedom at the time.

Unruly young Nez Perce braves drank "firewater" that they had gotten from settlers. Braves had earlier prepared for war by purchasing guns and ammunition from the whites. Walaitits, a brave whose father had been killed by the white man, cried for revenge. Someone urged Walaitits to go and kill the white men who had murdered his father. Walaitits, Red Moccasin, and Swan Necklace drank until they were intoxicated. The three braves became belligerent and readied for war. These were all members of Chief White Bird's band. Joseph and Ollokut were gone during this incident.

Braves rode to the Salmon River and Slate Creek on June 13, 1877 and lay in wait behind rocks, where they shot Richard Devine in his open doorway. Next, they rode to the village of John Day, shooting Henry Elfers, Robert Bland, and Harry Beckroge dead. The Nez Perce War had begun. When they returned, White Bird jumped onto his horse and rode through the camp, urging his braves to carry out more raids.

Toohulhutsote, who had been jailed by the army, joined the insurgents and went out to kill and plunder with the others. These actions had sparked the initial phase of the Nez Perce War. Many of the tribe returned to Lapwai Reservation. Joseph wanted peace and to return to the reservation. Ollokut remained silent. Three Eagles said that he could not go back and would fight. It was too late. The damage had been done.

The settlers, hearing rumors of the Indian war, began making preparations. The settlers at Slate Creek were undermanned with few firearms. There were 40 women and children and only 23 men. They hurriedly built a stockade and decided that someone should go for help.

Tolo (Alanewa), wife of Tawe (Red Wolf), a peaceable Indian woman, was elected. Tolo traveled the 25 miles to Florence, a mining town, and cried for help. She returned with twelve armed miners to Slate Creek. A monument near Grangeville was later erected in her honor.

The tribe had to eat, so Joseph and his chiefs moved into White Bird Canyon where they rounded up their cattle for butchering. White Bird Canyon was very grassy with steep rolling hills. The terrain was uneven with buttes, knolls and ridges. The creek ran through the bottoms.

General Howard had sent to Fort Vancouver and Fort Walla Walla for more Cavalry and infantry units, which were moved by steamship up river to Nez Perce Country. At Fort Lapwai troops received rigid training in Indian fighting. On June 15, two companies under Captain Perry arrived at Fort Lapwai from Fort Vancouver.

On June 16, Perry and companies F & H, a complement of 98 men, departed Fort Lapwai for White Bird Canyon. The soldiers had lost much sleep, being in the saddle for days. It was drizzling rain as they rode first to Cottonwood and on to Grangeville.

As Joseph's scouts observed the procession, it was no surprise to them that the soldiers were coming to fight. The U. S. Cavalry, led by Captain Perry and his militia and scouts, arrived in White Bird Canyon at about midnight the evening of June 16.

At dawn the next morning June 17, 1877, Captain Perry, his two companies, eleven volunteers and scouts rode down the steep hill into the canyon, a 3,000 foot descent to creek level. About 300 yards out, troops led by Lieutenant Theller saw six Nez Perce Indians on horseback moving toward them, carrying the white flag of truce.

A rifle crack broke the silence, then another, as Ad Chapman (Theller's scout) fired two rounds that struck the dirt near the flag bearers. Horse-mounted Indian observers scattered, returning fire. It was a stand-off. Perry's men and volunteers fired on the Indians and began the bloody clash.

Nez Perce warriors stripped down to loin-cloths and moccasins for war, according to their tradition. Joseph, on the other hand, remained in war-shirt, leggings, and moccasins for battle. Joseph had no choice, except to fight. An old Indian war slogan came true, "It is a good day to die." The Indians fought, seemingly with no fear, taking cover behind rocks and knolls, as did the militia.

Chief Joseph had allies in the Palouse people. Two major Palouse chiefs led their warriors. One was Chief Haltalekin (Red Echo) and the other chief was Husishusis Kute (Bald Head). He was a *tooat* or holy man. Husishusis led the ndians in the ancient Washani religion.

Lieutenant Theller attacked, followed by the volunteers. Joseph ordered the horse herd to be taken down to the river, behind the bluff. The women and children broke camp. Joseph divided his force into two groups under Chiefs Ollokut and Two Moons. They led the charge, attacking from two sides. Joseph blocked attack across the center. The army had cannons, Gatling guns, howitzers, rifles, pistols, and bayonets at their disposal during this campaign. The Indians had only 50 guns, bows and arrows, possibly lances, tomahawks, and steel or stone knives. Chiefs Too-hul-hut-sote and White Bird fought bravely.

The old Indian trick of stampeding horses through the enemy's ranks divided the soldiers. Soon, they were in disarray and confused. Horses ran free. Smoke and gunfire filled the air. Rifle cracks came nonstop. The Indians uttered shrill Indian warcries. The horses were spooked, so the soldiers had to dismount, causing Perry and his men began to retreat.

Chief White Bird pursued Perry and his men as they retreated to Cottonwood. Firing on them, White Bird followed them all the way to Johnson's ranch before turning back, to take spoils on the field. The Battle of White Bird Creek left 33 soldiers dead and 7 wounded.

General Howard, with 400 troops and 100 scouts, had left camp at Lake Tolo for Fort Lapwai. On the 23rd of June, he sent Trimble and his men to Slate Creek to defend the citizens. The general awaited word of the whereabouts of the hostiles and for reinforcements from Lewiston. Howard pushed his men from there to overtake the Indians.

On June 25th Howard split his column and advanced to Johnson's ranch. Upon reaching Grangeville, he was joined by Perry and his remaining troops, Howard advanced to White Bird Canyon.

Joseph had fewer losses. Joseph's Nez Perce had the victory, delivering the second most severe defeat to the army since the Little Big Horn. At this juncture, people feared that Joseph would conquer Howard and unite with the Columbia Plateau Indians and become unbeatable. The Nez Perce War was underway.

Joseph returned to his lodge to learn that he had become a father, a daughter had been born. Chief Looking Glass arrived with more warriors. Joseph had begun an exodus that would continue for days, weeks, and months. Chief Looking Glass was camped on Cottonwood Creek. He pulled up stakes and moved to the Clearwater, trying to avoid war. That night the Indians held a victory dance. The following day, in a brilliant tactical maneuver, Joseph exited White Bird Canyon in a wide circle, making tracking them very difficult. Using this method, Joseph avoided contact with Major Green's three companies of Cavalry and twenty Bannock scouts, coming from Fort Boise. The army did not engage Joseph and his warriors again until Cottonwood was reached. The chiefs had nearly 300 warriors to lead into battle, on June 22nd.

On June 26th, at White Bird Canyon, the rain had washed the dirt from the shallow graves, exposing the dead soldier's bodies. Howard had them reburied. The corpses had been stripped of clothing, but Joseph's warriors had taken no scalps. As Howard reburied the dead, Captain Paige climbed to the crest of a high ridge. From that viewpoint he

Chief Joseph's Warriors during the Nez Perce War
Public Domain

surveyed the Indians, beyond the Salmon, retreating. Miles arrived at White Bird. On July 9 Howard followed Joseph's path of retreat.

Joseph had made camp at Horseshoe Bend and prepared to cross the Salmon River. Ollokut and White Bird also wanted to cross the Salmon and flee to out distance the general. These chiefs had the mind-set that if they could escape Howard's jurisdiction, they would be free of war. The tribe was joined at Horseshoe Bend by Five Wounds, Rainbow, and other Nez Perce warriors who were back from the buffalo hunt. The chief council planned their defense. Howard, with 700 Cavalry and Bannock scout, Buffalo Horn, pursued the Nez Perce on June 28. Joseph crossed the Salmon River, baiting the General, to cut off his supply lines.

Five Wounds and Rainbow remained behind, with other warriors set as snipers, to slow Howard down. This was on the afternoon of June 28th. The snipers began taking pot-shots at the soldiers as they approached the crossing; until the soldiers returned fire with their long-range rifles. The Indians disappeared. Where Joseph's people had crossed with little trouble, Howard had a tough time with all the big guns and supply wagons. Joseph re-crossed the river at Craig's Ferry where he attacked Howard from the rear, causing the General many losses. Joseph made a temporary treaty with the soldiers, trading supplies with them.

With Howard on the move, many more of Joseph's tribe went back to the reservation. Others shifted into the camp of Chief Looking Glass, who was camped on the Clearwater just 4 miles south of Kooskia. Many braves had left there to join the hostiles. Getting wind of this, Howard ordered a surprise raid on the camp of Chief Looking Glass.

Captain Whipple and his complement rode to the camp, hoping to capture them and take them to Mount Idaho. The soldiers reached camp at dawn. Chief Looking Glass came to meet them displaying a white flag. When Whipple asked the chief to surrender, White Bird refused, and one of the Captain's men began firing on the camp.

The Indians returned fire, and Looking Glass joined them as they retreated, shooting back. Looking Glass joined Joseph and addressed the chiefs, vowing to fight the Bluecoats. Looking Glass had sent word to the Indian agent that he and 40 warriors wanted to come in to the Lapwai Reservation. Howard's order and the attack by Whipple and his men caused the chief to revert from being peaceable to a warring Indian. Looking Glass's band proceeded to join Joseph on the Clearwater River. Meanwhile, some of his braves told some Chinese workers that they were declaring war on the white man and would commence to raid on the Clearwater in 48 hours. Because of the threat, Mount Idaho sent out 20 volunteers to the Clearwater.

The army in the meantime was close behind Joseph's braves. Joseph traveled from Craig's Mountain to Cottonwood and camped two miles north of there. He positioned warriors on both sides of the road.

Capt. McConville was riding hard from Slate Creek to reinforce Whipple's command. July 4th, Indians ran from his soldiers at Norton, acting fearful; however, McConville had been ordered to take a different route. Had he followed the decoys, they would have been ambushed.

Captain Whipple had sent Lieutenant Rains and his detachment to scout for Joseph's Nez Perce on the same day. He was to report back if they found anything. Instead, Rains and his men rode right into Joseph's trap. Caught in the crossfire, the soldiers dismounted and ran for cover. The ambushed soldiers dropped one by one from the warrior's bullets, until all were dead. Joseph lost 9 braves in the skirmish at Cottonwood.

When Whipple arrived he knew from a distance that he was too late to save them. He placed his men in combat position not far from the massacre site. The same day, the hostiles attacked Whipple and his troops at Cottonwood House.

Perry and his troops waited hours for another attack. Instead, Joseph's warriors had attacked Mount Idaho. On July 5th the Indians sent up smoke signals, in three billowy puffs, from a plateau about three miles away. Randall and Evans attempted to break through the hostiles lines. They both were killed. McConville arrived too late to save Randall. On July 6th, to prevent a massacre, Simpson and Whipple rode with their complement to the citizens' rescue. On July 9th, some warriors again attacked Mount Idaho and fought Major George Shearer's men. Howard had done a reversal, turning his troops about. He ordered a night march to join Perry reaching Grangeville in time by July 9.

During the retreat, Chief Joseph had led his whole village, beginning with an estimated 750 tribes-people. There were 400 warriors, who mounted a massive herd of splendid Appaloosa horses into battle. The Nez Perce had bred and raised the beautiful Appaloosa. Their herd count reached 2,000 head, along with other breeds, and pack mules. Horse-drawn travois pulled lodge-poles, carrying goods, hides, and infants. As their horses were lost or stolen in battle, the Nez Perce rounded them up and stole more to replenish their stock.

Thinking they were far ahead of Howard's army, Joseph made camp and rested near Cottonwood Creek at the Clearwater River, where he joined Looking Glass. Their horses grazed on the grassy hillsides. They fished and hunted to fill their bellies, while young braves raided small farms stealing cattle and horses. The Indians held a pow-wow and war dance. They played stick games and raced their horses. By accident a few volunteers discovered the unsuspecting Indians in their leisure. This was on July 11th across the Clearwater River. They surveyed the Indians holding horse races, as part of their festivities. The Battle of the Clearwater ensued. Toohoolhootsote led 24 warriors across the river to meet Howard's attack. Other braves rushed to join Toohoolhootsote.

Howard had 400 men and 182 scouts. The soldiers dug in and built rock barriers. Howard ordered the attack, led by Perry and Whipple on their right and left flanks. The hostiles were caught in the middle. The Indians caught one line of soldiers in their crossfire. 400 soldiers rushed to their aid.

The Indians met the charge. Joseph rode along his lines, giving war-cries and encouraging his warriors to fight. White Bird did the same. Their voices could be heard above the din. One warrior appeared on a ridge in rifle range, dancing and waving a red blanket, touting the soldiers. During the melee the Indians chanted eerie death and scalp chants. Rifle fire and howitzer bursts showered the Nez Perce. Indians continued their shouts and warcries through the night.

At dawn when the pack-trains arrived the Nez Perce were quick to attack, killing two. Indians made sallies on foot and horseback. The fighting was heavy. A cloud of acrid gun-smoke shrouded the field. War-cries and rebel yells filled the air. During the fighting a calamity occurred, when Company B and the 21st Infantry behind the two mistook each other for the enemy. They began firing on their own allies. Finally

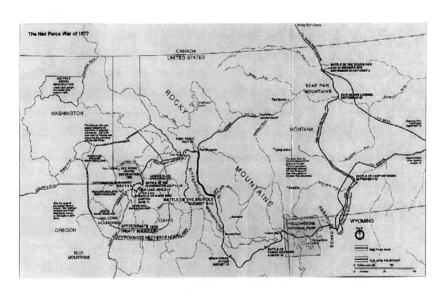

Nez Perce War Battle Map
Public Domain

Lieutenant Leary of the 4th Artillery ran out between the two lines with his rifle held by two hands in the air, shouting "Cease fire." Miller and Perry made an assault on the spring held by Indian snipers on July 12th. The men's canteens had gone dry, and they were parched. The army gained control of the spring. There was a heavy barrage of fire that afternoon, but the soldiers pushed the Indians back. The fighting lasted over 30 hours, and the warriors succeeded in defending their camp.

Captain Miles arrived with 200 more men. Joseph had been overseeing the women, packing up the goods and teepees. With Miles arrival, Howard had 600 soldiers to face 100 Nez Perce warriors.

Howard launched a full frontal charge. Their backs to the deep and swift Clearwater River, the Indians fled in retreat, leaving food cooking and lodges standing. In all Howard suffered 13 dead and 23 wounded, while Joseph claimed four dead and six wounded. The Nez Perce were outnumbered six to one. Howard still had the upper hand with Gatling Guns and Howitzers versus Joseph's warriors' Winchesters.

On July 13th Howard's Cavalry appeared on the bluffs overlooking Kamiah Valley. They rode down to the water's edge, where the last of the hostiles had completed crossing the deep and swift Clearwater River. Joseph's snipers fired on the soldiers across the river. Militia returned fire with Gatling guns and rifles. The snipers scattered the Cavalry with their bullets, giving Joseph enough time to escape.

Joseph broke camp four miles from Kamiah, and sent a messenger to Howard, asking for terms of surrender. He said that he did not want to leave the land of his father's or to bring misery on his people.

The chiefs then sent No Heart, a Nez Perce warrior, under a white flag, to speak with Howard about terms of surrender. Howard returned to Kamiah after hearing the news. The messenger and his wife surrendered.

The Nez Perce began their ascent up the Lolo Trail over the Bitterroot Mountains. The trek has been referred to as the Nez Perce' "Trail of Tears" for the hardships and struggles that they faced.

On July 16th, Joseph met his tribesman Red Heart as he was returning home from the "buffalo hunt" on the Upper Missouri. He did not join Joseph, but continued to Lapwai. Howard captured the group

General Howard during the Indian War of 1877
Public Domain

and claimed he had taken them prisoner at the Battle of the Clearwater. Howard's men stripped the peaceful band of personal belongings, guns, and horses. Joseph's people were marched to Lapwai and Fort Vancouver; where they were held until spring.

Joseph held a tribal council on the Weippe Prairie, at the start of the Lolo Trail. Chiefs Looking Glass, Too-hul-hut-sote, and White Bird wanted to join the Crow Indians in "buffalo country." Looking Glass was convinced that they should escape to the land of the Crows, but he was a dreamer. The Crow Indians had long been the enemies of the Nez Perce, yet he thought them to be their allies. Joseph refused to leave, not wanting to abandon "The Land of his Fathers" and Old Joseph's wish. They accused him of cowardice. Actually Joseph was very brave and far from being a coward. Joseph was overruled, yet was established as the true leader to lead the people to Canada. He made Pile of Clouds his war-leader. It was decided that messengers would be sent to chiefs Charlotte and Michel of the Flatheads and the Pend d'Oreille to attain permission to pass through their country in peace.

About three miles from what is now Orofino, in Idaho Territory, forty or fifty warriors held back as a rear guard. A trap had been set by the Nez Perce. Trees had been sawed as obstacles to drop cross their path of retreat. Major Mason almost fell for the ambush, but a rifle shot from McConville's troops warned them of trouble in the area. One of his scouts was found dead, two injured and two more were taken captive.

As the Nez Perce traveled down Lolo Canyon, their progress was impeded by an obstruction. A bulwark, named Fort Fizzle, blocked their path, on July 25th. The structure had been built by Captain Charles C. Rawn with the help of 44 soldiers. The structure was built three feet high, and a rifle trench was dug. It blocked the trail access to the Bitterroot Valley. He recruited about 100 settlers and 30 additional soldiers to guard against Indians.

Rawn held a council with Joseph, White Bird, and Looking Glass. The chiefs had friends in Montana and had traded at Missoula. They said they wanted to pass peacefully and no one would be hurt. Rawn would accept their proposal only if they surrendered and turned over their arms, ammunition and horses.

The chiefs refused the offer. Captain Rawn wanted another council on the next day. He would not otherwise grant safe passage. Looking Glass and a few braves met with him the next day, with no answer resulting. Looking Glass said he would have an answer the following morning but Joseph knew that Chief Charlotte of the Flatheads would not come to their aid. The farmers left for their homes. The Nez Perce did not want to fight them. The next day Captain Rawn heard the Indians singing, high on a ridge along the side of the cliff, as they moved in single file over the mountain. They had fooled Rawn. The Indians mused about the ruse as they rode along toward the Bitterroots.

In the Bitterroots, the Nez Perce bought coffee, flour, sugar and tobacco from merchants. In Stevensville one merchant would not sell to the Indians, but other shop owners profited more from his refusal. They used money for their transactions. The hostiles crossed Lolo Creek and ventured up a grade onto the Weippe Prairie, where there was water and grass. Some braves returned to Kamiah following Major Mason for several days as he pushed toward Missoula.

Joseph's Indian warrior Cavalry were extremely adept at stealing horses and combat. The braves began rounding up horses from Joseph's strays and stole ponies from peaceful Indians in the valley until they had rounded up a herd numbering 700 horses. These braves burned homes in Kamiah and stole livestock.

Howard assigned Major John Green's complement from Fort Boise to guard the Camas Prairie. He ordered more troops from Georgia and Washington Territory. Howard's personal command consisted of Captain Miller's 21st Infantry. Four companies were headed by Captain Evan Miles and four companies served under Major Sanford. Howard rested at Kamiah before continuing in pursuit of the hostiles. He had left half of his troops there, taking the remainder to pursue Joseph. The ascent above Kamiah with wagons and heavy guns was rugged with slippery trails, undergrowth, rocks, and fallen timber, a 16 mile trek.

Believing that they had won the fight, the soldiers began to burn the lodges, but White Bird's warriors drove Gibbons back. Joseph engineered breaking camp and loading the pack-horses. His warriors captured Gibbon's cannon and ammunition. They disabled the howitzer

125

Nez Perce Chief Looking Glass
Photo Courtesy of Wikipedia.org

and left it lay. The braves started their own fire that raged toward the soldiers in the strong wind, but the wind changed directions and the fire died out. By evening, 29 died. Gibbons and 40 soldiers were injured.

As General Howard arrived, the Indians disappeared. Joseph had lost twelve at Big Hole, including women and children. Two of his wives were among the dead. Looking Glass's daughter was slain and some of the best warriors were killed, including Rainbow and Five Wounds. Ironically, two of the three that had first initiated the rebellion, Walailtits and Red Moccasin Tops, died there also. After burying his dead, Joseph continued his flight. He rallied his braves on higher ground out of rifle range and gathered up a number of ponies that had scattered during the fray. The Indians departed Big Hole Basin and crossed back into what is now Idaho and Lemhi Canyon. Chief White Bird held council with the Shoshonis. He attempted to petition them to ally with the Nez Perce against General Howard. Being traditional enemies of the Nez Perce, the Shoshonis refused the offer.

Howard received word that the hostiles were now raiding ranches. and leaving the carcasses of the cattle they slaughtered as they lay. The Nez Perce surrounded a ranch at Horse Prairie Creek. The settlers put up a fight, but eight men were massacred. Chief White Bird was blamed for the attack. The braves stole a keg of whiskey, which may have accounted for their actions. General Howard attempted to cut off the renegades, who were headed for Yellowstone. He sent Lt. George Bacon and forty men to intercept them at Targhee Pass. Captains Calloway and Norton arrived from Virginia City to reinforce General Howard's column.

The Big Hole fight was on Looking Glass' watch, and he lost face for maintaining lack of security. Leaning Elk assumed his duties. After the Battle of Big Hole, the Nez Perce held council and decided to raid Howard' s camp for horses at Camas Meadows on August 17th.

General Howard's men were tuckered so he pushed hard to reach Camas Meadows where they could camp and rest. With a heavy guard posted, the men had a false sense of security. Two Nez Perce had been seen milling around, but nothing was thought of it. In reality, they were

Joseph's spies watching their every move. One hundred fifty soldiers bivouacked for the night, thinking the Indians were a day's march away.

Joseph's scouts apprised him of Howard's position. 40 Nez Perce warriors stole in during the night, tricking the guards as they entered the camp. The sentry thought them to be soldiers. Joseph's warriors cut loose the mules before being discovered. The Indians did not answer the sentry, so he discharged his weapon, awakening the camp. Warcries broke the silence, as the braves stampeded about 150 mules by waving buffalo robes. The surprise caused pandemonium in the darkness. In the confusion, the men clamored to dress, searching for their guns and ammo. A bugler blew the call to attack.

The Indians drew fire as they rode out. Howard ordered his officers to recover the mules. Captains Carr, Jackson, and Norton took chase after the renegades to recapture the mules, which were far ahead of them. Carr led the advance, attacking the warriors with the mules. As Jackson and Norton joined Carr, the Indians initiated heavy resistance.

Cunning Joseph stationed snipers on all sides to surround the Cavalry. The ensuing soldiers had to reign up, even though Norton was in trouble. Major Sanford called retreat. Lieutenant Benson stood for a moment and received a bullet through his buttocks. Carr recaptured the mules, but lost them again. The bugler blew retreat, as the other troops under heavy cross-fire withdrew.

Joseph's double-flank movement succeeded. His warriors picked off many off the soldiers who were trying to reach their horses some 500 yards away. Norton still engaged in fighting. It took Howard's full complement to rescue them. Seeing his advance, the Indians retreated. The army covered about 20 miles before returning to camp. Howard then pursued the hostiles, who now had a three day lead. Joseph continued along the Lolo Trail, against the Rocky Mountains, toward Yellowstone.

W.T. Sherman, General of the Army, was in Yellowstone Park during a tour of the western forts. He was escorted by Lieutenant Colonel Gilbert and two troops of Cavalry from Fort Benton, which was near Great Falls. General Sherman left the park, narrowly escaping a confrontation with the Nez Perce hostiles.

As the fugitives rode through Yellowstone, they encountered the Cowan party. They were tourists that had come to view the geysers from Helena, Montana. The Indians broke up their wagon and stole the camp equipment and supplies. Although the chiefs wanted to free the tourists, the unruly braves shot Cowan and left his body lying by the trail.

Another group of tourists in the Weikert party left Helena for Yellowstone Park. The renegades shot Mr. Weikert through his shoulder-blade while riding his horse. His mount stumbled on a log, throwing him.

Weikert still held his pistol and jumped to his feet, firing at the warriors. He remounted, still firing as the braves ran toward him. In the meantime, they pillaged the camp, stealing 14 horses, the blankets, tents, and saddles. The red-skins proceeded to burn anything left over. The hostiles killed Mr. Kenk and stole a wad of bills from Mr. Stewart, but spared his life. Those of the party that escaped made it to safety. Some arrived at Mammoth Springs, nearby and two continued 150 miles to Virginia City, Montana. Howard was never under manned. He always had scouts keeping him informed and used the telegraph to track Joseph.

Military companies dispatched from around the country were constantly coming to join the fray. By keeping his numbers of fighting men up, Howard was never overpowered.

Howard sent a currier to Sturgis, instructing him to travel at top speed along the Yellowstone River in an attempt to detain Joseph's Nez Perce, but the message arrived too late. In the interim, the Nez Perce killed two mountain men and a boy that Sturgis had deployed to reconnoiter. The trail of the renegades was discovered along the Stinking Water River. Looking Glass had ridden ahead to council with the Crow Indians, who chose neutrality. A scout told Joseph that Sturgis was ahead and that the prairie was on fire. The Indians continued on toward Canada.

The Nez Perce at this time numbered 400 warriors strong. Joseph sent a group of his braves toward Hart Mountain, dragging bundles of brush behind their horses, hiding their tracks.

Sturgis led the 7th Cavalry after them "post haste." When Sturgis vacated, he left a clearing large enough for the Indians to travel through, as Joseph had planned. He eluded both Howard and Sturgis at Clark's Fork. Sturgis had been tricked. The officers decided that the lieutenant would still pursue the Indians. Colonial Sturgis intercepted him at Canyon Creek by traveling west along the Yellowstone, and the Battle of Canyon Creek ensued. Canyon Creek was a dry wash, surrounded by ten to twenty foot walls. The hostiles began firing from both sides of the canyon on September 13th, but two of Sturgis' companies drove the Indians back. They fought hard to regain ground and defend the women and children.   Sturgis ordered Benteen to lead his Cavalry around the hills and across the creek to try and cut off the horse herd. He then ordered Merrill's battalion to protect Benteen's left flank.   As the Cavalry rode out, the Nez Perce anticipating their move, peppered them with bullets. The soldiers dismounted. Lt. Otis advanced on foot with his "Jackass Battery." The Nez Perce drove them back. Sturgis' plan had backfired.

Captain French's Company M gave boisterous yells, as they rushed up the hillside in an effort to reach the Indians. Some were on horseback, others on foot. Seeing a group of warriors in a huddle, the soldiers fired directly on them, killing some.

The 7th Cav. advanced onto the valley floor and was met with a barrage of Indians' bullets. The sniper fire pinned them down. Joseph had held Sturgis. The soldiers made camp, being exhausted. During the night, Joseph's Nez Perce broke camp and continued their retreat. With the Army's advantage of howitzers, 21 Nez Perce died, while the Army lost 3, with 11 wounded.

The next day, Joseph's people entered "The land of the Crows." It was not the paradise that Chief Looking Glass had hoped for. Instead, it was another fight. Their old enemies, the Crow Indians, had been expecting them. A running battle began that stretched over 150 miles of hard fighting. The Nez Perce lost nearly 900 spent horses that day. The Crows continued to fight them within 40 miles of the Musselshell River.

Nez Perce braves commandeered a stagecoach and burned the way station and buildings. The young bucks took turns driving and riding on and in the coach. The braves toyed with the stage until they became bored, when they destroyed it and burned the mail. The driver and the passengers escaped into the brush hoping to be rescued by Howard. The Indians had outdistanced Sturgis and his soldiers. They traveled along the Musselshell River, while Joseph made a wide sweep west around the Judith Mountains. On September 23th, they reached the freight depot on Cow Island.

The Nez Perce crossed the Missouri River and attacked the garrison. It was sheltered by a small earthwork structure, guarded by Sergeant William Mulchert, twelve soldiers of the Seventh Cavalry, and four citizens, who defended over 50 tons of supplies (both government and private).

The goods had been recently unloaded from the Steamship Benton onto the bank of the river. The steamer had departed down the Missouri a short time before the Nez Perce raid. At one time, Joseph offered to surrender for 200 bags of sugar, but was asked to surrender anyway. The Indians stole the sugar. The hostiles helped themselves to all of the supplies that they wanted and burned the remainder. The "Skirmish at Cow Island" lasted 18 hours; two volunteers were wounded.

Major Ilges and 36 volunteers left Fort Benton for Cow Island. On September 25th, Ilges began tracking the hostiles up Cow Creek Canyon. Lieutenant Hardin brought soldiers down river by boat. After travelling ten miles a scout located the Indian encampment. The insurgents had surrounded a wagon-train near Judith Basin.

As the soldiers arrived, the Indians set fire to the wagons as seven emigrants fled into the hills. The Nez Perce rode down the canyon for about one half mile, attacking the troops. As they left, the warriors broke off into small groups and disappeared.

Major Ilges and his men had taken cover. From the high ground the Indians initiated rapid fire. The fracas started about noon, and for two hours they fought. The Indians were terribly accurate with their rifles, without showing themselves. They ceased firing from the front.

Major Iges suspected a rear offensive and retreated to Cow Island. Snipers held them down until the main body of Nez Perce warriors escaped. One citizen and a horse had been killed, while two Indians had been injured. Joseph anticipated no opposition through the buffalo country. Miles got the idea to shell the bluff with big guns in order to signal the steamship to return. The Benton and crew returned to Cow Island Crossing.

Chief Peo-peo-hi-hi-h (White Bird)
Public Domain

Chief White Bird and Jimmy Hayes
Public Domain

The end of September 1877, the Nez Perce camped along the Milk River, aided by ample drinking water and firewood. The tribe had enough time to rest. Horses could graze and gain back the weight they had lost from constantly being on the move or in battle. They had plenty of antelope, buffalo, and deer to provide their meat supply and winter robes. The Indians could relax with Howard far behind them. They built up their winter stores on the Milk River, rested and tended their wounds.

They continued, reaching the vicinity of the Bear Paw Mountains, 1300 miles from Wallowa Valley and just 40 miles from the Canadian border. Rain mixed with snow as the tribe faced the task of finishing the last leg of their journey into Canada. There Joseph and his twelve year old daughter readied their horses and adjusted the loads, anticipating their quest.

Out of nowhere from the south rode a line of Cavalrymen charging the camp. Fifty or sixty braves guarded the horses. Miles had the advantage, with 600 Cavalrymen, infantry, and his Cheyenne Indian scouts. His complement was equipped with a breech-loading Hotchkiss gun and a twelve pound Napoleon cannon. Miles used a double line of the 2nd and 7th Cavalry in an attempt to divide and conquer in a single charge. Joseph and his daughter were cut off from the camp. He gave her a rope and told her to tether the horses before joining the others who were isolated. Joseph broke and ran through the melee. Reaching his lodge, his wife handed Joseph his rifle and urged, "Go and fight."

Miles' column caught Joseph, splitting his ranks. His brother Ollokut was killed. Joseph rushed to his family and though greatly outnumbered, the Nez Perce pushed the soldiers back. Miles held his ground. The Cavalry stampeded the Indians' horses. Miles lost 26 men and 40 were wounded. Joseph lost 18 men and 3 women. If they had wanted to leave the women, children and the injured, they could have made it into Canada.

Chief Joseph finally sent Yellow Bull to talk with General Miles, who demanded surrender, assuring safe passage. At the time, Yellow Bull wondered if Miles was sincere. Some Cheyenne scouts spoke with Joseph and told him that they believed Miles truly wanted peace. Joseph met with Miles, but with no answer.

On the fifth day of talks on October 5, 1877, War Chief Joseph surrendered, giving up his rifle. He uttered those famous words,

"Hear me my chiefs, I am tired. My heart is sick and sad. From where the sun now stands, I will fight no more forever."

His flight for King George's land in Canada had failed. The long journey was over.

At the time, Gen. Miles had promised if Joseph surrendered, the Nez Perce could go back home. Miles and his troops escorted Joseph and his people to Tongue River, and taken to Bismark, North Dakota, against Miles wishes. Ordered to Leavenworth, Kansas and were forced to live by an unclean river. They bathed, drank and cooked from that river, causing many deaths.

From Leavenworth, they were shipped by rail to Baxter, in Kansas Territory; three died in boxcars. 70 Nez Perce died of exposure. Joseph told officials of Mile's promise to return to Wallowa several times , but was told that it was impossible. He and 150 of his tribe were exiled for a time in Indian Territory in Oklahoma. Lastly, they were shipped by rail to the Colville Reservation, in eastern Washington Territory.

Joseph and Miles always remained friends. Colonel Miles and his troops escorted Joseph and his people to Tongue River, but they were taken to Bismarck, against Miles' wishes and then ordered to Leavenworth.

Joseph's party was forced to live by a river that was unclean. They had to bath, drink and cook from the unsanitary river. Again, Joseph told officials of Miles' promise to return them to Wallowa, but it was not kept. He and 150 Nez Perce were exiled in Indian Territory in Oklahoma, and shipped by rail to the Colville Reservation.

Joseph never saw his Wallowa Valley again. Broken hearted, Chief Joseph died before his teepee fire September 21, 1904. Chief Joseph earned the respect of the officers who fought him, remaining close friends with General Miles, all of his life.

Miles was promoted to general over the Army. Joseph had met Buffalo Bill and traveled to Washington D.C. in 1897, and met President William McKinley.

Bear Paw Mountains Where Joseph Surrendered-
Photo Public Domain

Chief Joseph's Surrender in the Bear Paws.
Courtesy of Azusa Publishing, LLC

Joseph with his Famous Rifle-
Courtesy of Idaho State Historical Society

The Nez Perce Reservation is on the Columbia River Plateau, in Idaho, Oregon and Washington, and the Clearwater, Salmon and Snake Rivers. The reservation population was 17,959 tribes-people in the year 2,000.

The tribe has an Appaloosa breeding program. Fishers are active in tribal fisheries on the Columbia River, between Bonneville and McNary Dams; they fish for Chinook salmon and steelhead. The Nez Perce Tribe operates a fish hatchery on the Clearwater River. The largest town on the reservation is Orofino, in northeastern Idaho. The reservation headquarters is at Lapwai, Idaho. The Nez Perce (Nee-Me-Poo) National Historic Trail stretches from Wallowa Lake, Oregon, to the Bear Paw Battlefield near Chinook, Montana. It was added to this system by Congress as a National Historic Trail in 1986.

ᴧᴧ◇ᴧᴧ

The Nez Perce loved to tell stories and hear stories told. The sagas retold again and again were legendary mythology. One of their favorite narratives was how Coyote created human beings. Coyote is the trickster figure of the Nez Perce tribe. These stories were the delight of young and old.

How Coyote Created Human Beings

One day, long before there were any people on the Earth, a monster came down from the North. He was a huge monster and ate everything in sight. He ate all the animals, the chipmunks and the raccoons and the mice, and all the big animals. He ate the deer and the elk and even the mountain lion.

Coyote couldn't find any of his friends anymore and this made him very mad. He decided the time had come to stop the monster.

Coyote went across the Snake River and tied himself to the highest peak in the Wallowa Mountains. Then he called out to the monster on the other side of the river. He challenged the monster to try and eat him.

The monster charged across the river and up into the mountains. He tried as hard as he could to suck Coyote off the mountain with his breath but it was no use. Coyote's rope was too strong.

This frightened the monster. He decided to make friends with Coyote and he invited Coyote to come and stay with him for awhile.

One day Coyote told the monster he would like to see all of the animals in the monster's belly. The monster agreed and let Coyote go in.

When he went inside, Coyote saw that all of the animals were safe. He told them to get ready to escape and set about his work. With his fire starter he built a huge fire in monster's stomach. Then he took his knife and cut the monster's heart down. The monster died a great death and all the animals escaped. Coyote was the last one out.

Coyote said that in honor of the event he was going to create a new animal, a human being. Coyote cut the monster in pieces to the four winds. Where each piece landed, some in the North, some to the South, others to the East and West, in valleys and canyons and along the rivers, a tribe was born. It was in this way that all the tribes came to be.

When he was finished, Coyote's friend, Fox said that no tribe had been created on the spot where they stood. Coyote was sorry he had no more parts, but then he had an idea. He washed the blood from his hands with water and sprinkled the drops on the ground.

Coyote said "Here on this ground I make the Nez Perce. They will be few in number, but they will be strong and pure." And this is how the human beings came to be."

The Nez Perce Legend of the Seven Devils Mountains

Long, long ago when the world was very young, seven giant brothers lived in the Blue mountains. These giant monsters were taller than the tallest pines and stronger than the strongest oaks.

The ancient people feared these brothers greatly because they ate children. Each year the brothers traveled eastward and devoured all the little ones they could find. Mothers fled with their children and hid them, but still many were seized by the giants. The headmen in the villages feared the tribe would soon be wiped out. But no one was big enough and strong enough to fight with the seven giants at the time.

At last the headmen of the tribe decided to ask Coyote to help them. "Coyote is our friend," they said. He has defeated other monsters. He will free us from the seven giants.

So they sent a messenger to Coyote. "Yes, I will help you," he promised. 'I will free you from the seven giants.'

But Coyote really did not know what to do. He had fought with giants. He had fought with monsters of the lakes and monsters of the rivers. But he knew he could not defeat seven giants at one time. So he asked his good friend Fox for advice.

"We will dig seven holes," said his good friend Fox. *"We will dig them very deep in a place the giants will always pass over when they travel to the east. Then we will fill the holes with boiling liquid."*

So Coyote called together all the animals with claws—the beavers, the whistling marmots, the cougars, the bears and the rats and mice and moles—to dig seven holes. Then Coyote filled each hole with a reddish-yellow liquid. His good friend Fox helped him keep the liquid boiling by dropping hot rocks into it.

Soon the time came for the giants' journey eastward. They marched along, all seven of them, their heads held high in the air. They were sure that no one dared to attack them. Coyote and Fox watched from behind some rocks and shrubs.

Down, down, down the seven giants went into the seven deep holes of boiling liquid. They struggled and struggled to get out, but the holes were very deep. They fumed and roared and splashed. As they struggled they scattered the reddish liquid around them as far as a man can travel in a day.

Then Coyote came out from his hiding place. The seven giants stood still. They knew Coyote.

"You are being punished for your wickedness." Coyote said to the seven giants. *"I will punish you even more by changing you into seven mountains. I will make you very high, so that everyone can see you. You will stand here forever to remind people that punishment comes from wrongdoing. And I will make a deep gash in the earth here, so that no more of your family can get across to trouble my people."*

Coyote caused the seven giants to grow taller, and then he changed them into seven mountain peaks. He struck the earth a hard blow and so opened up a deep canyon at the foot of the giant peaks.

Today, the mountain peaks are called 'The Seven Devils.'
The deep gorge at their feet is known as Hell's Canyon of the Snake River. And the copper ore scattered by the splashing of the seven giants is still being mined there in that area.

Bannock Warriors
Photo Courtesy of the Idaho State Historical Society

CHAPTER NINE
THE BANNOCK WAR

Northern Paiutes (*Numa*) lived south and west of the Shoshoni in now Oregon and Nevada. They were the "Water Ute" (from across the water). An offshoot of the Northern Paiutes, they would become known as the Bannocks. The story was passed down from their ancestors about how they had traversed a long way across the water to arrive on this continent. They were taller in stature than the Shoshoni, and more light skinned, like the Nez Perce. A source of the word Bannock was two Shoshoni words, bamp (hair) and (nack) backwards motion or *Bampnack*, translated (Bannock). They called themselves *Pah'ahnuck*, translated Bannock and *Numa*, meaning "the people." Shoshonis called them the *Ba-naite*, the "people from below."

Bannock hunters were far ranging across much of what became Idaho, Montana, Nevada, Oregon, and Wyoming. Millions of bison once roamed the Snake River Plain. As the buffalo began disappearing from the base of the Blue Mountains, the Paiutes (Piutes) crossed the Snake and followed behind the migrating herds north into present day Idaho. Boise headwaters begin in the Sawtooth Mountains, flow across Idaho, empty into the Snake, Columbia, and into the Ocean.

They had split off as an offshoot of the Northern Paiute and emerged as the Bannock. The Bannock took up residence on the Salmon and intermarried with the Salmon-eater (Lemhi) Indians. Others roamed eastward and impacted the Fort Hall Shoshoni Indians. Shoshoni (Snakes) first described the Bannock as one who always steals horses from me and called them "Robber Indians." Bannocks counted coup stealing Shoshoni horses; they were horse-mounted through the Shoshoni, by theft and then in trade. At first they stole Shoshoni horses then became friends, bonded, and intermarried, forming one people. They both spoke the Uto-Aztecan language; their dialects differed some. The Bannock dialect was closer to the Paiute language.

Raids to steal horses were led by a band chief. A ritual was held before a raid. The warriors held a buffalo robe while others beat it and chanted. The people gave them food and supplies for the hunt. Horses provided mobility to areas of subsistence. A useful buffalo horse or war horse was invaluable. The Bannocks were nomads on the Snake River Plains, who owned horses and lived in skin teepees. Bannocks were "hunters and gatherers" for subsistence. Horses drug travois loaded with teepees and goods. Bannock Indians received horses in trade, became part of the horse society, and served as middle men trading ponies to the Cayuse and Nez Perce to the north. It was not uncommon to see Bannock, Nez Perce and Shoshoni camped together. Bands lodged in extended family bands with no head chief. A communal leader may have been director of dances, hunts and war. Composite band members were unrelated, seldom numbered over 30, and did not have societal clans.

Male Bannock Indians wore war shirts of two deer skins, breech clouts, leggings worn from knee to the ankle and moccasins during warfare. They painted their faces with colorful war paint. Women wore dresses, leggings and moccasins. They made dresses of two elk skins and their leggings reached the knee. Women wore deer hooves, bird bones, rabbit toe and clam shell earrings bartered from Coastal Indians, also ear and lip plugs. Body piercings were common. Colored clay was applied to the face and skin for adornment. Women wore intricate chin tattoos.

In the fall, hundreds of salmon amassed in the streams to spawn. Paiutes built two piles of stone called weirs across the river to form a trap to catch the salmon; they used harpoons, baskets, nets or by hand. Paiutes left Fort Hall and moved along the Snake River, below Shoshone Falls to fish for Chinook, where schools of salmon amassed that failed to climb the falls. They fished the Snake River past the confluence of the Boise, Payette and Weiser Rivers to the Salmon River. Salmon was their main staple. Bannocks subsisted on fish, roots and game. John C. Freemont recorded seeing Salmon-eaters fishing at Shoshone Falls.

The Bannock painted their favorite war horses for battle; one mark was a black handprint on the horse. They were strong warriors in battle, armed with rifles or bows and arrows, fierce in battle, who engaged the Blackfeet in war, scalped them, and counted coup. Many guns and scalps were taken. The Bannock Indians fought any Blackfeet. Back in camp they performed the victory dance or scalp dance.

Moonlight raids were opportune. They delighted in stealing enemy's horses and building up large herds. Wealth was measured in the horses they owned. They often raided enemy bands to retrieve horses that had been stolen from them.

The Blackfeet Indians were so named because their moccasins were blackened from walking across the burned prairie.

In early autumn, Bannock families moved up to the hills onto the Camas Prairie. Bannock banded together with the Fort Hall, Lemhi and Sheep-eater Indians. Squaws dug camas root and ground it in mortars with pestles into flour to make Indian bread. In late autumn they returned to Fort Hall to prepare for the buffalo hunt when the buffalo were fat.

During Indian summer, pine nuts were harvested. A ritual was performed and Indians danced for three nights. As the dance ended, they bathed to cleanse themselves; the shaman said a prayer to the Great Spirit for a good harvest. Pine nuts were good fresh and roasted, ground in mortars into flour, mixed with water and made into gravy or were stored below pine boughs for the winter. Nuts were scattered in gratitude to the gods. Teepees were erected in a large circle. They danced in unison.

Hunters targeted antelope, bear, buffalo, deer, and game for the band. Parties hunted antelope and deer on horseback in the fall, when they were meaty. Pronghorn antelope (*hutsa*) herds ranged in the hundreds. The "Desert Deer" was known for its speed and ability to flee.

Buffalo hunters left Fort Hall under the direction of the hunt leader. Bannock hunting parties rode in large groups joined by their allies in order to ward off bands of warring Blackfeet or Crow Indians, who would attack at any time to steal their horses.

After a good hunt, pack mules were used to carry the buffalo meat and robes back to camp. As the season changed from autumn, the Bannocks winter camped with the Fort Hall Shoshonis. Huge buffalo herds that grazed on the Snake River Plain completely vanished from around Fort Hall after 1840.

Chiefs Tahgee and Buffalo Horn led parties to the Upper Missouri to hunt buffalo and rode through the Tahgee Pass, Yellowstone and Clark's Fork across the Continental Divide to the Upper Missouri and the Plains. Sometimes the Crow were friendly with the Bannock and traded with them and other times they fought. The Bannocks and Flatheads were normally allies, but other times squabbles occurred over horse theft.

Settlers confused Bannocks with Paiute Indians. Most Fort Hall Bannocks were mean spirited and did not much like the white man and would rather raid the white men than befriend them. Bannocks disliked palefaces on their lands and rarely invited them to hunt buffalo. They expected the white men entering their camp to observe customs and smoke the pipe with them. If the palefaces ignored these, they fought. The fierce, warlike Bannock Indians were disliked by the settlers.

The Bannock Indians made an exception and traded directly with Jim Bridger and Captain Benjamin L. Bonneville. Chief Washakie sometimes interpreted for Bridger with the Indians. Immigrants visited Fort Hall and estimated the Bannocks Indians' numbers at nearly 1,000.

The Bannock Indians hunted with and wintered among the Shoshoni Indians. Their numbers were estimated to be around 1500. Fort Hall Shoshoni were friendly to the white man.

The Hunt Party left St. Louis and paddled up the Missouri in dugout canoes. On August 1804, Pierre Dorian was introduced to Lewis and Clark on the Missouri by his father, Pierre Dorian, Sr.

Marie was an Iowa Sioux Indian born in a teepee on the banks of the Missouri River, who married Pierre Dorian, Jr., a French-Sioux Indian cross. Wilson Price Hunt needed an interpreter in 1811. Pierre Jr. spoke Sioux and signed on with Wilson Price Hunt in St. Louis as interpreter.

Reaching the Green River Valley they traded with Shoshoni for jerky, hunted buffalo and jerked two tons of meat. Crossing the Hobart River Valley Basin, the party sank their dugouts in the Snake and rode over the Continental Divide. They rode southwest on horseback to Jackson's Hole and hiked out of the Teton Range. Four traders stayed to trap beaver near Three Forks, the spring of 1812. A Crow war party killed one of the trappers.

Two Shoshonis guided them across the Snake River, up Fall Creek over Teton Pass and again crossed the divide. They rode horses to

Pierre's Hole and floated in dugouts down the north fork of the Snake to Henry's Fork. They lost canoes and a man drowned at Caldron Lynn. Hiking three days without water on the Snake River Canyon, Marie suffered from exhaustion and thirst.

They reached Hagerman Valley, and found precious drinking water. Hunt's party had made it over the Rockies! Near Eagle, Idaho they met Shoshoni Indians who shared fresh puppy meat with them. Some tribes scoffed at eating dog meat. Spent horses were sometimes eaten in the absence of food. Even Lewis and Clark ate horse flesh at "Colt Killed Camp."

Pierre traded the Indians for a much needed horse and had to dismount and surrender the horse to Marie and the boys. Two famous women, Marie and Sacajawea once met briefly, in 1811, as the Manual Lisa Party overtook the Hunt party. Marie and Sacajawea conversed momentarily.

The party split into three groups led by Hunt, McKenzie and Crooks who reached Astoria, May 11, 1812. Their fur shipments to Great Britain were jeopardized by the War of 1812.

In 1813, Pierre and Marie returned to the mouth of the Boise River working for Reed in the Astoria group. Reed's post was erected on the eastside of the Snake.

Reed abandoned the original Fort Boise (cabin) since unruly Bannock Indians often demanded guns, and built the lean-to Dorian, La Chapelle, Le Clerc, and Rezner lived in to hunt beaver. In 1814, a band of warring Bannocks burned down the cabin, now abandoned and continued down the Boise, out of control, whooping and chanting war-songs. Marie was skinning beaver at Reed's cabin, 15 miles east of the burned cabin, north of the Boise River near present day Notus, Idaho.

An Indian squaw informed Marie that a band of warring (Dog-ribs) Bannocks was coming up river. She took her two boys and rode up stream to find Pierre, camped two days because of bad weather, saw a Bannock Indian smoke signal coming from Table Rock (Ala-Kush-pa) a plateau Indians used to send smoke signals, and waited another day.

Marie discovered Le Clerc just barely alive. He related to her the details of the massacre; she hoisted him up onto her horse, but he continually fell off. Approaching the cabin, Marie saw a band of Indians gallop off on horseback. Despite her help, Le Clerc died. She buried him under snow and brush. As Marie entered the cabin, she saw her husband's scalped and mutilated body, Reed, and the others.

The boys were hungry not having eaten in days. Marie built a fire, returned to the cabin armed with a knife and a tomahawk and saw wolves eating their kill. She scared them off, found fresh fish in the cabin, hurried to the boys, and cooked the fish. Now Marie must care for her boys alone. She mounted her horse and crossed the Snake River to begin her long trek to Fort Astoria, leading her horse over the snow covered Blue Mountains. Marie built a fire under an overhang; the boys were warm in their rabbit-fur robes. They ate berries, nuts, and rabbits.

When her resources ran out, Marie killed the horse for food and plodded westward, her papoose in a cradleboard strapped to her back. She held little Baptiste's hand and trudged along.

Marie was snow-blind and exhausted as they reached the Umatilla Indians, who rescued them. The Umatilla brought them to their village and cared for them. They had withstood the long trek and now were safe. Marie began a completely new lifestyle in Oregon, remarried and started over.

In 1862, gold was discovered in the Boise Basin. Miners infringed on Indian land and found gold on the Nez Perce Reservation and Black Hills. The gold-rush to Idaho City, Silver City, Coeur d'Alene River and Salmon River opened up mining as thousands of miners migrated to Idaho Territory. Lewiston's Tent City was named capital. Idaho City was a boom town with the largest population in the northwest.

George Grimes led prospectors from Auburn, Oregon Territory in July of 1862 and hired Bannocks as guides into the Boise Basin. Six miles from Bannock (present day Idaho City) near Centerville they struck gold, but the Bannocks killed George Grimes.

The Saga of Bigfoot began with a mixed-blood Cherokee Indian traveling west. Starr Wilkinson was a 6 foot 8 inch, 300 pound half-

146

breed, son of a Cherokee-negro mother and a white father. Wilkinson claimed to be from the Cherokee Nation. He began his trip west in 1856 from St. Louis by wagon-train.

He loved a girl, named Jesse Smith, who jilted him for her new lover, Mr. Hart, an artist from New York. Wilkinson caught Hart and Jesse lying in the sagebrush and fought with Hart, dragged him into the Snake River and drowned him. Wilkinson panicked and fled. While on the run, he joined a renegade Paiute band; they called him "Nampa" in Paiute (Bigfoot). He became their chief. The wagon-train returned to St. Louis, due severe cold. On the return trip, Nampa's band massacred the passengers including his Jesse Smith and burned the wagons.

He led the renegades on stagecoach raids, along Reynolds Creek, on the Boise-Silver City road. On these raids the man (who never rode a horse) ran alongside the moving stage coach, giving war-whoops, putting fear into the passengers. They robbed stages near the mining town of Silver City in Idaho Territory. Army investigators detected a bare seventeen and one half inch footprint along the Weiser River. The story of a mysterious giant appeared in the Idaho Statesman Newspaper with an offer of "$1,000.00 REWARD, DEAD or ALIVE for BIGFOOT."

In 1868, as Nampa ran alongside the stagecoach, John Wheeler, a bounty hunter, was poised in a nearby grove of Aspen trees with his 44 caliber long-rifle sights on him. He fired his repeating rifle. Bigfoot disappeared. Then Wheeler espied a tumble-weed moving along the ground and commenced firing. The hulk ran wildly toward him.

Wheeler claimed he shot Bigfoot 16 times and apologized for killing him. Bigfoot told Wheeler his life story, in exchange for giving him an Indian burial. He was just 30 years old. The folk-hero, Paiute Chief Nampa was the namesake of Nampa, Idaho. The "Bigfoot" legend didn't end there. Rumors are his ghost still roams the Owyhee desert.

Chief Tendoy, unable to attend the Fort Bridger Treaty of 1868, sent Taytoba, his sub-chief to represent him. Taytoba signed the treaty, but General Augur did not know Taytoba was Lemhi and not Bannock, which disqualified the signature. Separate negotiations were conducted in Virginia City, Montana. On July 3, 1868, Tahgee, 800 Bannocks, and hundreds of Shoshoni met at Bridger to sign the treaty for a reserve. The Bannock's word was good; they kept the peace from 1863-1868.

Hoping to keep their tradition, Bannock Chief Tahgee insisted on retaining the Camas Prairie as part of the reservation and to be able to continue to hunt buffalo. The Army clerk recorded his request, but wrote down "Kansas Prairie," instead.

The Fort Bridger Treaty made division between the Eastern Shoshoni (Goshiute) of Utah and the Western Shoshoni (Wihinasht), the Boise, Bruneau, and Weiser Shoshoni. The Salmon-eater and Sheep-eater Shoshoni were referred to as the Northern Shoshoni Indians. The Western and Northern Shoshoni all lodged in Idaho Territory.

The treaty made revision for a Shoshoni Bannock Indian reservation. The Fort Bridger Treaty of 1868 was signed by President Andrew Johnson of the United States of America and the Eastern Shoshoni and Bannock tribes of the Territory of Utah. General W.T. Sherman and other U.S. Army officers signed the treaty.

Bannock Indians that signed the 1868 Treaty of Fort Bridger were Tahgee, Taytoba, Wertzewonagen, Cooshagan, Pansookamotse, and Awiteetse. Shoshoni Indians that signed were Washakie, Waunypitz, Toopsepowot, Narkok, Taboonshe, Bazeel, Pantoshega and Ninnybitse. Each made his mark to sign.

In 1868, the Sioux Indians drove the Bannock and Shoshoni tribes out of Yellowstone. In August of 1868, both the Bannock and Shoshoni Indians were camped long the Boise River. They were allowed to hunt the buffalo come autumn. In 1869, the Sioux Indians went on the war path and killed 29 Bannock and Shoshoni Indians.

The Bannock hunted buffalo with the Eastern Shoshoni in the Wind River Mountains. On route home, they stopped at Fort Hall to receive their presents. While they were there, Chief Tahgee told the Indian Agent that they were ready to move to Fort Hall. Before they left the reservation for Fort Hall, Tendoy, the last Lemhi Chief and sub-chiefs made their marks to ratify the removal agreement, but 2/3's of the bands' signatures were lost and the government could not produce them.

On the twenty third of April, 1869, Agent Powell escorted 850 Bruneau River, 300 Boise Shoshoni and 150 Bannock Indians from Boise to the Fort Hall reservation. On July 30, 1869, President Grant gave the executive order to grant the Bannock Indians a home at Fort Hall reservation in Idaho. The Governor was informed of the decision and passed the word to the Indian Commissioner. The U.S. Army moved other Indians onto reservations by 1870, confiscated their guns and shot their horses to limit their movement. Hostiles were relocated onto government reservations.

The Indian Appropriation Act was passed which removed government recognition of tribes as independent political entities. For 200 years, horses revolutionized the Amerindians' world. The horse and Indian era was a good one. Indians loved their horses, but the romance between the horse and Indian was short lived.

During the bitter winter of 1869, the Lemhi did not receive any appropriations. Chief Tendoy led 700 Indians of his band to Virginia City, Montana and made demands to the Governor of Montana for a reservation for his people on January 3, 1870.

Tendoy and his four sub-chiefs met with Governor Ashley and three of his staff. Under the agreement, signed by the chiefs, he appointed A.J. Smith, a long time friend of the Indians, as Agent to represent them in Washington to secure settlement on the Lemhi River. Tendoy requested bullets to hunt buffalo in Montana to feed the Lemhi.

In 1871, the government sponsored the wholesale slaughter of bison herds to force the Plains Indians onto reservations. Bison were slaughtered by the thousands.

On February 12, 1875, President Grant established the Lemhi Valley Indian Reservation for the exclusive use of the mixed tribes of the Bannock, Shoshoni, and Sheep-eater Indians. The reserve was 100 square miles for Sacajawea's people on the Lemhi River. There were mixed feelings about funding the Lemhi Indians.

In 1877, 600 Bannock Indians dwelled at Fort Ross on the Upper Snake River in southeastern Idaho. One hundred fifty miles to the north, 150 Bannocks shared the Lemhi Reserve with the Sheep-eater and Lemhi Shoshoni and were dissatisfied with the food quality and reservation life. Game had become scarce because of the paleface hunters.

The Bannock were never too fond of the white man. August 1877, a Bannock brave wounded two white men. In November, a white man was murdered. The Indians protected the killer. An attempt to arrest the warrior resulted in 53 Bannock braves arrested. Col. John Smith captured their arms and horses. The Bannock warriors on the reservation rebelled. On May 30, a Bannock brave killed two palefaces.

In 1877, the Indian Wars were dwindling. In 1878, Chief Buffalo Horn and his Bannock braves became angered when some settlers brought their hogs to the Camas Prairie to graze. The pigs had done considerable damage to their prairie land. This event caused the Indians to rise up. Buffalo Horn's Bannock warriors visited the camp of the white men. They injured one man and threatened another. Because of broken treaties, Buffalo Horn prepared for war, while Chief Tendoy's band chose peace and rode to the Lemhi River Reservation. Buffalo Horn's band of 200 Bannocks went on the warpath attacking cattlemen on the Camas Prairie killing two, a third man hid in the brush, another fled on horseback to bring word of attack to Fort Boise and U.S. Army Captain Bernard.

The marauders plundered wagons near King Hill, stealing arms, and fled across the Snake River by using the ferry. Reaching the other side, they cut it loose. The Bannocks then killed some settlers at the mouth of the Bruneau River. Captain Egan along with 46 Bannocks and Weiser Indians joined Buffalo Horn. His band increased to 300.

Bernard's column pursued Buffalo Horn over the divide to the headwaters of the Owyhee River. Some 20 volunteers, stationed at Silver City, reached the hostiles first and engaged them, meeting heavy fire. They retreated in a running battle; Chief Buffalo Horn was killed in the siege on South Mountain. Buffalo Horn's body was later buried at Good Shepherd Cemetery at Fort Hall Indian Reservation, Bingham County, Idaho, U.S.A.

Egan replaced Buffalo Horn, and their numbers grew to 800, as others joined them, outnumbering Bernard and his men, three to one. There was a rumor circulating that Chief Buffalo Horn had lived and escaped to Wyoming.

Howard left Fort Walla-Walla for Boise June 9, 1878 and by June 18th, had raised 900 troops, with six officers and artillery to handle the outbreak. Captain Bernard and several other excellent officers joined General Howard's columns to engage Egan's band.

During the Bannock War the hostiles took Chief Winnemucca and the Malheur Paiutes at the reservation captive, taking their blankets, horses, and weapons. When Sarah Winnemucca learned of her father's plight, she rode to Sheep Camp, desperate to find her father.

She met with Army General Howard who gave her a letter of safe passage. Picking up the Bannock's tracks, Sarah rode after them. From a high overlook Sarah surveyed the Bannock camp of several hundred teepees.

At nightfall she descended the slope, concealed under a blanket and war-paint. Sarah entered the chief's tent. During the night, she ushered her father out of camp and was joined by her brother, his wife and two cousins, who had come to help. They held the horses and aided in their escape to Sheep Camp. From there, the army escorted Sarah, her father, and entire family to Fort McDermott and safety. Sarah and her sister-in-law later worked for the army as couriers.

The marauders meantime rode toward the John Day River, in Oregon Territory, killing ranchers and stealing livestock. They rode along the Grand River into the Blue Mountains. Hostiles were made up of Malheur, Paiute, Shoshoni, Umatilla, and Weiser Indians. The savages continued their rampage, killing and pillaging; they moved fast covering hundreds of miles. The rebels fought, whenever the Cavalry overtook them. They kept the renegades on the run.

Captain Egan crossed the Columbia River, offering the Umatilla Indians 2,000 horses to join them in battle, but they refused and the rebels opened fire on them. This time the Umatilla warriors offered to join them and began firing. They killed Captain Egan. With both chiefs dead, the hostiles scattered. With some still on the rampage, the remaining insurgents crossed into Idaho Territory, attacking whites on the Salmon River and Payette Lake. They continued into Montana.

Miles engaged the renegade Bannocks in 1878. In an early morning raid Captain Miles, with 75 Cavalry plus Crow Indian scouts, managed a surprise attack on the hostiles, killing eleven. This attack ended the war. Nelson Miles was promoted to General, as Commander-in Chief of the U.S. Army, in 1895.

Captives were taken from Fort Omaha and Fort Hall to Fort Simcoe, Washington where Captain Winter delivered 600 Indians. Heavily armed riverboats picked up some along the Columbia River. Captives were imprisoned or released. Some of the Bannock Indian captives were transported to Fort Hall Indian Reservation.

Just nine soldiers died, 24 wounded. 24 citizens were killed and 34 wounded; there were seventy eight Indian deaths, 66 were injured.

War Chief Buffalo Horn
Led the Warriors in the Bannock War of 1878
Photo by Public Domain

Photo of the Grave of War Chief Buffalo Horn
Photo Courtesy of David Habben

Shoshoni Indian Chief Pocatello
Photo Courtesy of the Idaho State Historical Society

CHAPTER TEN
THE SNAKE WAR

A real need for a military fort became apparent as Indians constantly raided wagon trains and stage lines. The army planned to build a centrally located military garrison in the Boise Valley. The Shoshoni Indians did not like the white man crossing their lands. Consequently, the Snake Indians harassed the settlers in wagon trains. In October 1851, Snake Indians killed eight men at Fort Hall Idaho.

The following event led to the fort being built. A wagon-train headed west for Fort Boise along the Oregon Trail, in August 1854. The Ward party of 23 people decided to have a picnic on the Boise River, south of president day Middleton, Idaho. They had unhitched their wagons, when older brother, Robert ran in shouting, "the Indians have stolen a horse." Hitching up their horses, the Ward party pulled their rigs onto the road, trying to escape, but they became surrounded by 200 renegade Snake Indians (Shoshoni). Alexander Ward, their leader, was shot and killed instantly. Arrows and bullets flew, as all hell broke loose. By sunset, all adult males in the party had perished.

Renegades attacked the wagons, women and children, stripping Mrs. Ward and her teen-age daughter naked. Possibly raped, the Ward women were slashed to ribbons with knives; their bodies seared with firebrands. Mrs. Ward was brutally bludgeoned to death, and her 17 year old daughter died, during horrific torture. Screaming in pain and horror, three little girls were burned alive. Three other children just disappeared. The savages burned the wagons and fled. The teen-age boys, both struck by arrows, crawled into the brush during the attack saving their lives. William showing much bravery, walked 20 miles to Fort Boise with an arrow through his lung. Hidden by sagebrush, Newton was later found alive.

At Fort Dalles, Oregon Major Rains ordered Haller and 26 soldiers to pursue the renegades. 39 volunteers, under Nathan Olney, with some Nez Perce and Umatilla Indians volunteered to ride behind the U.S. Cavalry. Arriving at the massacre site, Haller buried 18 bodies. Haller found the renegades' trail into the coming. Later they caught and lynched some of the attackers. General John Wool ordered Haller and 150 men back to the Ward Massacre Site in the spring of 1855. Haller took Nathan Olney, Indian agent, with him.

Gallows with nooses were built. Wagons were rolled out from under them. The renegades were hanged and cut down for burial the next morning. Haller rode with his detachment down the Boise, Payette and Snake Rivers, flushing out any of Ward's attackers to be hanged on the spot. Eighteen were hanged, the exact number killed in the massacre.

The Ward Massacre Memorial stands on the old Oregon Trail as a monument to the memory of the Ward family wagon-train just south of present day Middleton, Idaho and their memory on August 20, 1854.

In 1854, a Sioux Indian killed a Mormon's ox at Fort Laramie. Lt. Grattan led his troops into a Sioux village near the Platte River demanding vengeance. The Sioux killed Grattan and all his troops. The same year, the Ward Wagon train was massacred by a band of renegade Shoshoni Indians. The Modoc Indians rebelled in 1855.

Snake country massacres began as the Snake Indians attacked wagon trains, Army units and supply trains from 1854-1859. The Snakes were on the rampage from Utah into Oregon country. It was dangerous to be at Fort Boise or Fort Hall. Indian trouble closed both forts in 1856.

Pocatello was born in 1815 on the Raft River which empties into the Snake River. His given name was Tanaioza (pronounced Dono Oso) or Buffalo Robe. Pocatello's mother, Widzhebu was a Grouse Creek Shoshoni Indian and his father was a Flathead Indian named Cornell.

Pocatello is not a Shoshoni word, but it may have been a Flathead Indian name. Pocatello grew to be 5' 10" tall, a strong leader, who became chief of 300 Bear Lake Shoshoni Indians. His territory included Bear Lake, Bear River Valley and Raft River north to the Snake and the Great Salt Lake to the south. The California Trail routes: the Fort Hall, Hudspeth, Salt Lake and Oregon routes all cut through Pocatello's territory. Pocatello lodged between the junction of the California Trail and the Salt Lake Road. He rebelled against the hated white intruders that trespassed on their lands. By 1857, Pocatello was a young chief who controlled a huge territory around present-day Pocatello, Idaho. Pocatello rose to power and greatness in his band as a leader. Pocatello was a silent chief considered to be a hostile. Pocatello was greatly alarmed by the growing number of Mormons who were traveling north from Salt Lake City and settling in Shoshoni territory.

The Indians and Mormons increasingly clashed, with both sides committing brutal and unjustified murders. Pocatello was determined to resist white settlement. He led several attacks on the Mormons, killing many of them and stealing their horses. In 1858, General Johnston arrived in Utah Territory.

Settlers killed game where Pocatello's people hunted and used the water holes for their livestock, exhausting the supply. Cattle grazed grasses down to nothing and game could not forage. Settlers destroyed seeds Shoshoni gathered for food.

Pocatello hated to see his people starve during cold winters, so he camped near Indian Agent Brigham Young's camp. Young gave him food and supplies.

U.S. Army Colonel Patrick E. Conner and his company of 3rd California Voluntary Infantry Regiment were ordered to Utah to protect the Overland Mail Route and keep peace in the region.

Palefaces trespassed on Shoshoni lands; in 1859 there were numerous attacks along the Bear River, Cache Valley, City of Rocks, Hudspeth Cutoff, and Massacre Rocks all in Pocatello's territory A wagon train was attacked on July 26, 1859 at Twin Springs. In 1859, the Shepherd train was massacred south of Twin Springs. The following day, Snakes raided wagons at the Hudspeth Cutoff.

On August 31, 1859, Shoshonis massacred the Miltimore family in the American Falls vicinity. The Snakes made a series of raids on trains in eastern Idaho Territory. In 1859, two of Pocatello's warriors were killed by white men; Pocatello retaliated and sent out a war party that killed six emigrants.

In 1859, Chief Pocatello rode to Lieutenant Gay's camp. Gay arrested Pocatello and put him in the guard house. Major Lynde, Gay's commanding officer, released the Chief for lack of evidence.

Shoshoni Indian Chief Pocatello appealed to Eastern Shoshoni Chief Washakie to join him to go on the war trail against the palefaces, but Washakie was a peace chief and refused to fight the white man.

Even President Abraham Lincoln had heard of the famous Shoshoni Chief Pocatello.

June 23, 1860, a Shoshoni band attacked an Army road party in Malheur County, Oregon. October 16, 1860 renegades massacred the Utter Party west of Castle Butte in Owyhee County. On September 13, 1860, Snake Indians were responsible for the deaths of the Myers party of settlers at Salmon Falls in Idaho.

Palefaces trespassed on Shoshone lands, and in retaliation, Indians attacked the intruders. In 1860, a train was attacked in the City of Rocks. That fall, Shoshoni massacred the Utter train on the Snake and attacked the camp at Soda Springs in 1861. They stole livestock from the Harrison train in the City of Rocks.

August 9, 1862 emigrants traveled west. The Adams, Wilson and Kennedy trains followed the Smart wagon west. One half mile from Massacre Rocks, a war-party ambushed the Smart and Adam's train, massacred settlers, stole livestock and burned their wagons.

In the Utah Indian War, Indian war parties attacked the farmers and killed white men, women and children, scalping them. Pocatello's band captured women and children for slaves and wives. They burned the wagons and stole livestock. Slaves were captured in Indian fashion and they had taken captives from enemy tribes for years.

Gold was discovered in the Boise Basin in 1862. The army hoped to establish a military garrison in the Boise Valley, an extension of Fort Vancouver. Major Pinckney Lugenbeel was ordered to build such a post in Idaho Territory. Fort Boise was built in 1863 to protect the emigrants and miners. Camp River Boise, later known as Fort Boise was erected in 1863 next to Boise City.

General Crook made his headquarters there. As Indian Wars erupted a need for strong military garrisons was eminent. The Cavalry could be dispensed any time. With the Civil War winding down, Indian fighters arrived at the fort. The U.S. Army engaged the Indians in combat.

Miners rushed into the area with gold fever. In 1864 Boise City became the territorial capital of Idaho Territory. Boise grew at a rapid rate with the population explosion in Idaho from thousands of miners who rushed to the Boise Basin, during the "Idaho Gold Rush." Settlers came off the Oregon Trail into Boise the largest city on the trail. In 1864 Boise had 1,685 residents. The population of Idaho City was 20,000 people at the time.

The Treaty of Boise in 1864 was written at the fort. The simple document said that the Shoshoni Indians gave up the Boise River drainage for care under the U.S. Government and were treated as a favored tribe. The treaty was never legally ratified. At a later date Governor Caleb Lyon wrote another treaty with the Bruneau Shoshoni.

The Shoshonis had gathered for the traditional warm dance in Bear Hunter's village in January of 1863 to welcome the spring to come early and bless the bands with warm weather and abundance.

In 1863, the Bannock killed a white man, rumored to be an emigrant near Brigham City. Chief Snag and two braves came in to Brigham City to answer charges they had held a white captive, but the three Indians were shot down in the street at Bannock City by miners.

Meanwhile, Chief Bear Hunter's warriors did a war dance around the home of Mormon Bishop Preston Thomas, demanding wheat. The next day, Bear Hunter returned and was told the soldiers were near. Hearing that he could be killed, Bear Hunter stated that the soldiers might be killed, also. The chief rode to warn his people.

Colonel Conner rode to Bear River with an order for the Shoshoni to turn over the Indians responsible, but they would not turn in the culprits. Chiefs Pocatello had left the previous day prior to Conner's attack and took Sagwitch and other willing Shoshoni with him to safety. Chief Bear Hunter and other sub-chiefs refused to join Pocatello and vacate camp, taking Colonel Conner's demands lightly.

Colonel Conner stated that he planned to take no prisoners of those that resisted. His plan was to chastise the Utah Indians for their wrong-doings. Colonel Conner marched at night from Salt Lake, in order to provide the element of surprise. Two Cavalry units marched at once. The town of Preston, Idaho heard of the approaching troops.

Conner left Salt Lake by nightfall. At dawn, January 29, 1863, they swam their horses across the icy cold Bear River, one mile south of

Bear Hunter's camp nestled in a ravine. The Soldiers appeared, dismounted and the fighting began.

One hundred Bannock warriors fled to the hills. The fighting lasted four hours. Bear Hunter and 250 Indians were estimated dead, including women and children. The Army lost 23. Soldiers burned 75 teepees, captured 175 horses, and found 1,000 bushels of stolen wheat, leaving some for the Indians.

Conner was promoted to Brigadier General. A rumor reached them that Pocatello and his warriors were seeking a fight with General Conner and his troops, but when the Army answered, the Indians rode to the hills. Meanwhile, the Bannock Indians had moved into the Wind River Mountains.

After the Bear River Massacre, Colonel Conner attempted to capture Chief Pocatello, but to no avail. Chief Pocatello had escaped to the Green River region of Wyoming. The Bear River Massacre stopped the Indian attacks. Wagon trains crossed into Oregon unscathed. After the massacre chiefs Pocatello, San Pitch and their band were exonerated.

Conner rode to Fort Hall to remove any remaining hostiles. He left Salt Lake by nightfall with his Cavalry. At the Snake River Ferry, he came upon 17 Shoshoni lodges. They were peaceable, so Conner gave out gifts to the Shoshoni. If peaceable, he told them they would not meet the fate of those at Bear River.

Chief Winnemucca promised Agent John Burche of Nevada in May of 1863, that he would persuade Chief Pashego (*Pas-se-quah*) of the Nevada and Idaho Bannock tribe to attend a conference. Agent Burche met with the chiefs on the Humboldt River and Pashego, who promised no more attacks on the palefaces if the Indians were left alone, and promised to keep the peace. Chief Pocatello sent word via Washakie that he was ready to talk peace. Chiefs of nine Shoshoni bands, including Chiefs Pocatello and Sanpitch, except Chief Sagwitch, signed the Box Elder Treaty at Brigham City, Utah July 30, 1863.

An emigrant wagon train 40 miles west of Fort Hall was later attacked by Indians. Conner's Bear River massacre had made an impression and Indian attacks on wagon trains had slowed to a stop. Meanwhile, the Indians left to hunt the buffalo.

The Snake War (1864-1868) was fought between the United States of America against the Snake Indians. The term Snake applied to the Bannock, Northern Paiute and Northern Shoshoni Indians, who stretched across California, Idaho, Oregon, and Nevada. The Snakes continued to attack the white-eyes, mostly skirmishes. When volunteers went east to fight in the Civil War troops from California, Idaho, Oregon and Nevada provided protection for the settlers.

In October of 1864, General Patrick E. Conner arrested Chief Pocatello and transported him to Fort Douglas in Utah and charged him with theft. Pocatello was a brave leader of his people, feared by the military, Indian agents and settlers.

Pocatello stood up to Army officers. General Conner knew that Chief Pocatello was responsible for the recent raids in eastern Idaho Territory and planned to hang Pocatello. Utah Indian Agent O.H. Irish telegraphed President Abraham Lincoln and apprised him of Conner's intentions. President Lincoln was working on a peaceful resolve between the immigrants and the Indians.

When Lincoln learned of the actions against the chief, he directed the Secretary of War to telegraph General Conner not to execute Chief Pocatello. General Conner released Pocatello. Chief Pocatello liked to walk with various friends and their dogs just enjoying them. Chief Pocatello came out of his shell and even began to make friends among the white people. Chief Pocatello wore a discarded colonel's coat and a sword presented to him by an officer.

August 21, 1867, Governor Ballard spoke to the Indian chiefs:

"Now, are you willing to relinquish your title to all of the country you have claimed provided the government of the United States secures to you and your children, and to such other friendly Indians as maybe induced to go there on, the sole ownership of said reservation forever, supply you with subsistence until you can raise sufficient food for yourselves and furnish you an agent, teachers, books, implements of husbandry, etc."

Chief Tah-gee spoke, *"I thought when the white people came to Soda Springs and built homes and put soldiers in them, it was to protect my people, but now they are all gone, and I do not know where to go, or what to do."* The chief continued, *"The white people have come into my country, and have not asked my consent. And why have no persons talked to me before? I have never killed white people who were passing through my country. All the Bannock will obey me and be good, but the Sheep-eaters are not my people and I cannot be responsible for them. I will answer for the Bannock. The buffalo do not come as far south now as formerly, so we go further to the north to hunt them. The white people have scared them away."*

The Shoshoni Indians transitioned to the Fort Hall Reservation in Idaho in 1869 as well as 600 Bannock Indians.

The aging Chief Pocatello had been ill and in October of 1884, he was taken to the Snake River bottoms in Idaho, where he died. When Pocatello passed, he was buried in his regalia. Chief Pocatello instructed his people that he was to be buried in a huge spring with an unknown depth beneath the American Falls Reservoir. The Chief was interred in his garb, Army coat, guns, knives, and bow and arrows, all tied to his body. His 18 horses were slaughtered and buried with him to ride in the spiritual afterlife.

∧∧◇∧∧

In identifying various Shoshoni Indian bands the food that they ate at the time designated their name. The Shoshoni Indians had four seasonal rounds for different foods. Some bands subsisted on one particular food. The Sheepeater band made a steady diet of Rocky Mountain sheep as their main food supply and the top of the food chain.

Their Indian name was Tukadeka in Shoshoni translated to "sheep eater." The Sheep-eater Shoshoni were a rare band because they dwelled high among the rocky crags in the lofty mountains of Idaho, Montana, and Wyoming. The Sheep-eater Indians were known for their finely constructed bows, far superior to other ones. They were highly prized and their women tailored beautiful leather clothing.

Lewis and Clark had contacted the Sheep-eater Shoshoni in 1805. Lemhi Shoshoni Chief Cameahwait had spoken to Lewis of the "Broken Moccasin Indians," referring to the Mountain Shoshoni Sheepeaters. Possibly their moccasins were badly worn from scampering over jagged rocks.

162

In his journal, Lewis depicted the Mountain Snakes as poor, destitute wretches and described their fur clothing as gaudy. He said that they were flamboyant at times, boasters who told wild stories. Lewis said they were an honest fair and generous people and never beggars. Sheepeaters traded for guns and horses from the party.

It is hinted that the wild dogs of the Mountain Snakes were domesticated wolf pups. Lewis and Clark described seeing domestic dogs that looked like wolves that the Indians used to hunt elk. Domestic dogs were beasts of burden utilized to pull loads of goods and supplies by travois and haul firewood.

Dogs were kept as pets and watch-dogs. Puppies made a tender meal. Dog fur was woven into woolen blankets. Large dogs used for hunting looked like Russian wolfhounds. The bloodhound made good trackers. Two wolfhounds working together could cut a wild sheep from a herd and drive it into a crude corral.

Sheepeaters dwelling in the Yellowstone Mountains late in the 19th century were seen with at least 30 pack dogs. The pack dogs carried provisions, and skins. The Indians were armed with laminated bows and obsidian tipped arrowheads. Indians carried back packs and pack-dogs were commonly used. Sheepeaters also wove backpacks from strips of sagebrush bark constructed with skin or fiber straps. Food was wrapped in skins and carried on their backs.

The Sheepeater War was the last Indian War in the Pacific Northwest. At the time, there were around 300 Sheepeater Indians. The Sheepeater Indian Campaign took place mainly in Idaho. The events leading up to the conflict began when settlers in Indian Valley accused the Sheepeaters of stealing horses and killing three settlers near present day Cascade, Idaho.

August 1878, Shoshoni Indians were blamed for the deaths of two prospectors in an ambush at Pearson Creek five miles from Cascade. In February 1879, five Chinese were killed at Oro Grande mine on Loon Creek. Sheepeaters were blamed, although evidence was that white men, dressed as Indians killed them and began the Sheepeater War.

Two more men were murdered on the South Fork of the Salmon River, without evidence. General Oliver O. Howard thought the

Sheepeater were the last holdout of hostiles of the Bannock War giving him an excuse to pursue them.

Captain Rueben Bernard and Company G, 1st Cavalry, left Boise Barracks for Payette Lake (near present day McCall) riding pell mell north to intercept the warring Sheepeater Indians. Captain Bernard was under 1st Lieutenant Henry Catley of the 31st Infantry.

There were 20 Indian Army Scouts. Lt. Farrow rode east from the Umatilla Agency and 1st Lt. Catley rode south from Camp Howard to intercept the Indians. In the summer, the Army moved through the River of No Return in difficult terrain pursuing the hostiles.

In the first part of the war, the U.S. Army destroyed an abandoned Shoshoni camp. Then, the Army followed their trail despite warnings from Indian Army scouts and they continued to ride deeper into the canyon, where they were ambushed by two dozen Sheepeater Shoshoni Indians.

The following day the Indians set fire to the grasses at the base of the mountains below where the soldiers were camped. The flames leaped high and rose up the hill, but amid the smoke as it turned to darkness, the soldiers slipped past the Indians in the night, but they lost 21 pack animals and all their supplies.

On August 20, 1879, a Sheepeater Shoshoni war party of about a dozen braves attacked Army troops guarding a pack train at Soldier Bar on Big Creek. Corp. Charles B. Hardin and Chief packer Barnes and six troopers were on guard. They managed to drive the Indians off, with only one casualty, a private Eagan.

The summer of 1879, the Army moved to round up the Sheep-eater hostiles. The hostiles were pursued by the Army, led by Cayuse and Umatilla Army Scouts. After a difficult campaign and much searching, the Army discovered their locations. Those who chose war found themselves engaged with the Cavalry and their fight was short lived.

The militia battled a band of only 51 Sheep-eater Indians, just 15 of which were warriors. They had very few weapons, carbines, two muzzle loading rifles, one breech loading rifle and one double barrel shotgun. Outnumbered, the Sheep-eater Shoshoni surrendered.

Lieutenants Brown and Edward S. Farrow with twenty Army Indian Scouts negotiated the treaty, the end of October. The Indian finally agreed to transition onto the reservation. The final Indian War in the Northwest, the Sheep-eater Indian War was over.

The Fur Trade Era that began in 1670 was gone. The white man came in large numbers; their army overran the Indians. The American Indian Native fought a good fight, but war and smallpox took many thousands of the Indians' lives. Their world as they knew it was gone. Their battles over, the American Indians transitioned onto reservations.

W.A. Allen had an interview with a one hundred and fifteen year old Sheep-eater woman in 1913, meaning that she was born in 1798. Her Shoshoni name meant "The-Woman-Under-the-Ground."

The-Woman-Under-the-Ground told Allen that the Tukurikas (Sheepeaters) were driven south, into the hills and mountains by the Blackfeet Indians, which may be why they adapted to life in the mountain heights, forced to live among the clouds.

The Sheepeater woman said they hunted mountain sheep with their sheep-horn bows and arrows and used hunting dogs. The elder woman explained how her people lived in caves and overhangs. Instead of a teepee, they built wickiups high above their enemies.

The ancient one said that a wickiup was a cone-shaped hut constructed of cedar pole uprights thatched with grey moss and cemented with pine pitch. Flooring was of sheep skins. Their garb was made from skins of the antelope decorated with eagle feathers, ermine and otter skins.

Ancient one said that her people sometimes descended down to the valleys, but always returned to live high among the clouds. The one of great wisdom related how her people thrived on the mountain sheep and how the wapiti would ascend to mountain passes and the hunters would shoot them with their bow and arrows. They had excellent survival skills.

The remarkable account of the old woman from another era is simply amazing. She is a voice from the past and presents an interesting account of living archeology.

Sheep-eater Indians in Wickiup at a Mountain
Camp on Medicine Creek in eastern Idaho in 1877.
Photo Courtesy of the Smithsonian Institute

CHAPTER ELEVEN
INDIAN RESERVATIONS

The government forced the Indians to transition onto reserves, which was not easy for them. The government left the other tribes no choice, but to leave their traditional lands. Some Indians refused to make the move to the reservation. They wanted to remain on the lands of their ancestors and to fish, hunt, and gather like the old days. The Army considered them non-treaty or hostile Indians and were relocated onto government reservations. The U.S. Army moved most Indians onto reservations by 1870, confiscated their guns and shot their horses to limit their movement. The reservation was set apart for the Indians.

An Indian reservation is a land parcel given the government by the American Indian tribe through peace treaty. The natives do not have full power over the land, but they do have limited rule and want to rule by the unwritten traditional law.

Treaty promises were not always kept and the Indians suffered. Suddenly, their world was disrupted and change was introduced. The Indians' transition of lifestyle was a difficult act for them. It represented leaving the old traditional life way and learning the Christian work ethic and to be self sufficient.

In the beginning, the Indians had to depend on the government for food. The food supplies were late or inadequate and the people were hungry. Some of the Indians left the reserve to hunt. They hunted and fished.

The first Indian Reservation in America was established by President Ulysses S. Grant in order to help settle the conflict between the Indians and the settlers. Reservations seemed to be successful. The Indians had to transition from the hunting and gathering lifestyle to agriculture. At first, the Indians began to grow truck gardens producing vegetables. Farming was encouraged. In time, they began to plant and farm. Some failed, but over time they became successful farmers. The Indians purchased horses and cattle to begin ranching. Some tribes could hunt off the reservation. The chiefs received annual payments from the government.

Indian children were sent to boarding schools at Catholic or Protestant missions to be educated. The children wore identical uniforms. Their hair was cut short and they were not allowed to speak their native language.

Indians had their own councils, form of government, and even Indian police. The reservation Indians retained their old traditions, costumes, culture, dances, games, histories, songs, and stories. Annually, they held their powwows that were very festive.

Small communities were formed on the reservations. Businesses were built. Trading Posts and Tribal Offices were established, membership grew and reservation membership flourished. Some reservations have adopted legalized gambling with casinos and seem to make revenue through gambling casinos. Not every tribe has a gambling casino and not every state has a reservation.

Some reservations have been compared to Third World conditions. The members have allowed their neighborhoods to deteriorate and become run down. The monies that they receive are squandered and poverty conditions arise. The reservation takes on the appearance of a ghetto. Alcoholism is a scourge. Suicide is common.

A large percentage of reservation housing is inadequate. There is a need for housing. Less than 50% of bathrooms are indoors. An Indian Housing Authority exists, yet the need for housing is still not met. Forty nine per cent live in inadequate dwellings. Thousands of Indians are homeless or under-housed. Overcrowding is a problem. Three generations at times live in a two bedroom home. Facilities are sub-standard. Cooling and heating, kitchen fixtures and plumbing are often inadequate. Many Indians need pure drinking water and telephones.

Numbers of reservation members are unemployed and households earn only disability, social security, or veterans' income. Many employed Native Americans are earning poverty wages. Some households are overcrowded with too many occupants. At present, there are 300 Indian reservations in the United States. There is a need for health care. Some reservations have health centers, qualified physicians, and nurses and possibly a dentist. They have education centers, schools, high schools and training programs.

INDEX

BIBLIOGRAPHY

Addison, Helen and McGrath, Dan, War Chief Joseph, University of Nebraska Press, Caxton Printers, 1941.

Beal, Merrill D., I will fight no more forever. University of Washington Press, Seattle, 1977.

Chief Joseph, Chief Joseph's Own Story As Told by Chief Joseph in 1879 by Indian Culture

Madsen, Brigham D., The Bannock, University of Idaho Press, 1996.

Madsen, Brigham D., Northern Shoshoni, Caxton Printers, 1980.

Members of the Potomac Corral of the Westerners, Great Western Indian Fights, University of Nebraska, Lincoln, 1987.

Trafzer, Cifford E. and Scheurerman, Richard D., Chief Joseph's Allies The Palouse Indians and the Nez Perce War, Sierra Oaks Publishing, Sacremento,

Utley, Robert M., The Indian Wars, New York, The American Heritage Publishing Co., 1977.

Winnemucca, Sarah, Life Among the Paiutes, University of Nevada Press, 1883.

Wyman, Walker D, The Wild Horse of the West, Caxton Printers, Ltd. Caldwell, Idaho, 1945.

ELECTRONIC CITATIONS

<http://www.accessgeneology.com/native/nevada/northern_paiute_
indian_tribe_location.htm>

<http://www.backyardtraveler.blogspot.com/2009/02/tragic-path-of-
pyramid-lake-indian-war.html>

<http://www.carsonpedia.com/Paiute_Indian_War&oldid=44">

<http://www.digiital.library.okstate/encyclopedia/entries/1/1N018.html>

<http://www.en.wikipedia.org/wiki/Coeur_d'Alene_War>

<http://www.en.wikipedia.org/wiki/Palus_people>

<http://www.facebook.com/NevadaWar>

<http://www.galafilm.com/chiefs/htmlen/sauk/ev_badaxe.html/>

<http://www.legendsofamerica.com/na-bannock.html>

<http://www.militarymuseum.org/Owens Valley.html>

<http://www.national geographic.com/lewisandclark/record_tribes_
067_13_26.html>

<http://www.onlinenevada.org/articles/pyramid-lake-war>

<http://www.rootsweb.ancestry.com/~txbander/banderapass2.html>

<http://www.firstpeople.us/FP-Html-Legends/CoyoteCreatesHuman
Beings_NezPerce.html>

<http://www.xphomestation.com/paiutewar.html>

<http://www.3rd1000.com/history3/events/sheepeat.htm>

About the Author

Born in Lexington, Nebraska, Robert Bolen, B.A. has a degree in Archeology/Anthropology. In an Archeology class, he was informed that because of his Mongolian eye-fold, he was part Indian. In 1755, a Bolen ancestor was taken captive by Delaware Indians and later rescued with her baby daughter, Robb's Great, Great, Grandmother. When rescued, the poor girl (just 17) was scalped, but she lived. A French scalp was the size of a silver dollar. Family says she combed her hair to hide the scar and lived to be well over one hundred years of age. Bolen's served under George Washington in the American Revolution. In 1777, the author's ancestors erected Fort Bolin, near Cross Creek, Pennsylvania for protection from Indian attacks. Two ancestors were killed in Kentucky by Shawnee Indians allied to the British. Great Granddad Gilbert Bolen rode with the Ohio Fourth Cavalry in the Civil War under General Sherman. In 1866, Gilbert brought his wife and six children west to Nebraska in a Conestoga wagon. Gran-dad Denver Colorado Bolen knew Buffalo Bill Cody in western Nebraska. Bolen is an authority on Indian artifacts and glass trade beads. Robb and Dori Bolen reside in Nampa, Idaho, near Boise. Robb owns the website, Fort Boise Bead Trader.com.

176

More Books

by Robert D. Bolen

Smoke Signals & Wagon Tracks

American Indian Tribes of Idaho

Blackfeet Raiders
Nomads of the North

The Horse Indians

The Lakota Sioux Indians

The Medicine Crow Indians

"The Snake People,"
The Northern Shoshoni Indians

War Chief Paulina
& His Renegade
Band of Paiutes

The Paiute Indian Nation

Photos of Books Written
by Robert D. Bolen

THE LATEST BOOK WRITTEN

BY ROBERT D. BOLEN

THE PAIUTE
INDIAN NATION

by Robert D. Bolen

PHOTOGRAPHS COURTESY OF AZUSA Publishing, LLC

3575 S. Fox Street

Englewood, CO 80110

Email: azusa@azusapublishing.com

Phone Toll-free: 888-783-0077

Phone/Fax: 303-783-0073

Graphic Design Services

Provided by

DESIGNER

Cover Design

Book Layout

Text and Page Formatting

Editing

Photo Clarification and Enhancement

Etc.

Bonnie Fitzpatrick

208.249.2635

bjfitz 777@msn.com

H. 1/16

CPSIA information can be obtained at www.ICGtesting.com
Printed in the USA
LVOW06s2002171115

462996LV00007B/378/P